UNDERSTANDING THE POWER

of

COMMITMENT TO GOD

Simon Osamwonyi

Published in Nigeria by
Peculiar Household of Faith Fellowship
38 Adedoyin Street, Ajelogo Mile 12,
Lagos Nigeria.
Tel: 234-8167025183, 234-8058946026
Email: osascosi@yahoo.com
Skype: simon.osamwonyi

FIRST EDITION

ISBN: 978-978-960-911-6

CONTENTS

Dedication

To God Almighty, for giving the Word when I made inquiry from Him and for the inspiration to write; and

My late mentor, Dr. Dan Finch, who went to be with the Lord in January, 2016;

My wonderful wife and lovely children

Acknowledgement

First and foremost, I appreciate God for the opportunity to be a vessel, to deliver this word to the Body of Christ.

My deep appreciation also goes to my senior pastor, Rev. Obinna Egbuonu, for his leadership role in my life and encouragement in ministry.

Words cannot describe my gratitude to my beautiful and wonderful wife, Beauty, for being a tireless support at the home front and in the ministry. Dear, you have been a great source of reassurance and inspiration. I love you.

Finally, I do not take for granted, the many other people, who contributed in one way or the other to the successful completion and publication of this book.

May my God bless you all in Jesus 'name. Amen.

Preface

I am glad that this book, **Understanding the Power of Commitment to God** is coming at this time when the Church is seeing and talking about the need for us (members of the Body of Christ) to be committed to God in our service in His vineyard. Our commitment to anything we are called to do in life is always with benefits and blessings. The world is also talking about commitment in our career, job, academics, business, marriage, relationship, e.t.c.

The foundation of our commitment should be built on our commitment to God. Our commitment to God is not without blessings and benefits. God has said that whoever that is committed to Him will always share testimony. This is the foundation or the basis of writing this book. Our commitment to God should be examined from the point of faithfulness and intention (motives). Our intention for doing whatever we are doing for the sake of the Kingdom is very important. Our faithfulness to what God has asked us to do is important. I have also put into consideration that the grace of God is available to give to us what Christ died for. We should not rely on grace and not do anything to achieve what we want to be in life.

In writing this book, I am not undermining the fact that there are some believers who are passing through God's process of becoming what God desire them to be in life. That is understandable because I have and I am still passing through the process but during this time I still have some testimony to share for my commitment to God. God has not left me as an orphan, things may not be the way I wanted it to be but I am still able to meet some needs.

The question to ask is, how can we be committed to God that will bring the desired testimony? There may be some other ways to be committed to God, but I have presented the six that God taught me and instructed me to present in this book.

I want to encourage you to read this book over: keep it by your bed, underline the part that applies to your situation. Study it; use it, for this is not a "reading book "in the ordinary sense. It is written as a "guide book" to a new way of life.

INTRODUCTION

In 2005, while pastoring a church in Mile 12 area of Lagos state, Nigeria, I came in contact with a significant number of believers, who had been in Christ for many years, yet had little or no evidences to show that they were members of the Body of Christ. When asked to share their testimony, they had nothing tangible to point at that has really changed in their lives. For many years, they have had no jobs, no businesses, no good education, cannot afford to pay house rent, and of course feeding themselves and their families was a real challenge. Their lives were perpetual tales of woes -nothing positive had been going on for as long as they could remember.

I began to wonder whose fault this is. Is it that God refused to bless them or they are the ones that could not position and connect themselves in the path of heaven's blessings? I decided to seek the face of God. And this is what God told me: "**Anyone who will be committed to me will always have testimonies (blessings)".**When I heard this, I began to seriously examine the zealousness of these people and came to the conclusion that they were believers quite alright, but they had not been totally devoted to God. They paid a lot of lip service to the things of God but their faithfulness at times left much to be desired.

In the course of my time of reflection with God, He showed me six keys to pursue commitment to Him. They are what I will be sharing in this book. Of a truth, there might be some other ways, but these are the ones God has given me to share with the body of Christ.

I have to admit that there are many longstanding believers in such situations today. It looks like they are committed and serving God yet the state of their lives gives one concern. A five-year old child who cannot walk and talk will surely be a concern to his or her parents. In the same way, God, as a Father, is concerned about this set of people. God wants to deliver them and the time of their deliverance has come. The Bible says that upon Mount Zion there shall be deliverance and the children of Israel shall possess their possession and there shall be holiness (Obadiah 1:17).

You might also be at that juncture. You have probably been committed in some ways but might need to do more, or make some adjustment here and there, so that you can get the fullness God has destined for you. This book is written to help you move to your next level in life. It will serve as a guide, to help examine yourself –for any area(s) you may be falling short right now.

Sometime ago, I preached on these keys to commitment in a local assembly in Lagos and one of the sisters in the congregation decided to act on the words. A while later, she returned saying God confirmed His word with testimonies.

I urge therefore, that as you read, be ready to act on what God will say to you. The Lord will surely fulfill His word in your life too.

Joyous Reading!

Simon Osamwonyi

Definition of Key Words

"Moreover it is required in stewards that one be found faithful."

- **1 Corinthians 4:2**

The basis of this book is that as a steward, faithfulness is required.

Who is a Steward?

A steward is someone, who manages another's property or financial affairs; one who administers anything as the agent of another or others. Someone who has charge of the household of another, buying or obtaining food, directing the servants.

We are called as God's stewards to manage that which belongs to God. While God has graciously entrusted us with the care, development, and enjoyment of everything he owns, as his stewards, we are responsible to manage his holdings well and according to his desires and purposes. **For us to share testimony in our commitment to God, it is expected of us to be faithful.**

What is Faithfulness?

According to Wikipedia, faithfulness is the concept of unfailingly remaining **loyal** to someone or something and putting that loyalty into consistent practice, regardless of extenuating circumstances. It could also mean keeping to one's promises, no matter the prevailing circumstances. It also means to be reliable, steadfast and uncompromising.

We need to be faithful in our dedication to God with the whole of our heart. There is no secret hidden from God. Moses has the testimony that he was faithful in his entire house (Hebrews 3:2). Again when Nehemiah had to leave Jerusalem to return to Persian, he put Hanani and Hananiah in charge. The reason for his choice of these men was that they were "more faithful and God-fearing... than many" (Nehemiah 7:2).

When we consider unfaithfulness, the bible says in 1 Chronicles 10:13 that King Saul died for his unfaithfulness which he had committed against the Lord, for he did not keep the word of the Lord and also because he consulted a medium for guidance. May you not die because of unfaithfulness to God. I pray that you will be faithful in your entire house in Jesus name. Our motive is also very important.

What is Motive?

Motive is the reason for doing something.

As an individual, what was your motive for accepting Jesus Christ? Did you embrace the altar call just because you needed a job, good wife or good friends? I once met a young man that told me that the reason he gave his life to Christ was because the soul winner promised him a job. The moment he could not get the job, he left the church. When your motive is wrong, there will be no way you will share testimony in your acclaimed commitment. Your commitment must be of a pure and good motive. Do not be involved in eye service and never be men pleasers. What is your reason for paying tithe? What is your reason for sowing seed? Is your reason right or wrong? What is your reason for coming to fellowship? Are you there to worship God or to see friends and business partners? What is your reason for investing in the kingdom? Is it to get a hundredfold return? Your motive must be right in whatever you do in the Kingdom of God.

In proverb 21:2, the bible says that every way of a man is right in his own eyes, but the Lord weighs the heart. It is God that looks at the heart to determine the intention of doing anything. In 1 Samuel 16: 7, God told Samuel that the Lord does not see as man sees; for man looks at the outward appearance but God looks at the heart. So your intention matters in your commitment to God.

 An example of wrong motive in the scripture is in Genesis 11:1-6: "***And the whole earth was of one language, and of one speech. 2 And it came to pass, as they journeyed from the east, that they found a plain in the land of Shinar; and they dwelt there.3 And they said one to another, Go to, let us make brick, and burn them thoroughly. And they had brick for stone, and slime had they for morter.4 And they said, Go to, let us build us a city and a tower, whose top may reach unto heaven; and let us make us a name, lest we be scattered abroad upon the face of the whole earth.5 And the LORD came down to see the city and the tower, which the children of men builded.6 And the LORD said, Behold, the people is one, and they have all one language; and this they begin to do: and now nothing will be restrained from them, which they have imagined to do.7 Go to, let us go down, and there confound their language, that they may not understand one another's speech.8 So the LORD scattered them abroad from thence upon the face of all the earth: and they left off to build the city***". The people were of one mind and speech and this is pleasing to God. This is what we are looking for in the church today. Then why did God set confusion in their midst? Is God the author of confusion? NO. God set confusion in them because of their motive. They had a wrong motive to build the tower. Their motive was to make a name for themselves and not to exalt the name of God. Many of us today do things just for the sake of our own interest and glory. Our motive should be to bring praise and glory to God not ourselves.

Here are some specific questions to help us evaluate our own motives:

1. If no one ever knows what you are doing (giving, serving, sacrificing), will you still do it?
2. If there was no visible payoff for doing this, will you still do it?
3. Will you joyfully take a lesser position if God asked you to?
4. Are you doing this for the praise of others or how it makes you feel?
5. If you had to suffer for continuing what God has called you to do, will you continue?
6. If others misunderstand or criticize your actions, will you stop?
7. If those whom you are serving never show gratitude or repay you in any way, will you still do it?
8. Do you judge your success or failure based upon your faithfulness to what God has asked you to do, or how you compare with others?

Finally, the Grace of God

Grace can be defined as the unmerited or undeserving favor of God to those who do not deserve it. It is also the divine ability to carry out divine assignment. It is grace that gives us access to God. It is by grace we are saved. The grace of God is available, but we must not frustrate it. How can we frustrate the grace? When we refuse to do what is necessary. Apostle Paul says in **1 Corinthians 15:10**, *"But by the grace of God I am what I am, and His grace toward me was not in vain, but I labored more abundantly than they all, yet not I, but the grace of God which was with me."*

The labor of Paul paid off. He labored in the area of evangelism - **Romans 15: 20:** *"Accordingly I set a goal to preach the gospel, not where Christ's name was already known, so that I would not build on another man's foundation"* (AMP)

It was not by his power and might he was able to preach the gospel in the places where no one had ever heard the name of Christ before. It was the grace of God that helped him. He labored in the place of prayer for his converts. **Romans 1:8-9**," First, I thank my God through Jesus Christ for you all, that your faith is spoken of throughout the whole world. For God is my witness, whom I serve with my spirit in the gospel of his Son, that without ceasing I make mention of you always in my prayers;: Again in **Philippians 1:3-4** "I thank my God upon every remembrance of you, Always in every prayer of mine for you all making request with joy", Again in **Ephesians 1:16**,"Cease not to give thanks for you, making mention of you in my prayers". It was the custom of Paul to always intercede for the people he led to Christ. Was it by his power or might? NO, it was the grace of God.

It is through grace also that all these teachings in this book can be achieved.

What is Commitment?

Commitment is a promise to do something or to behave in a particular way. Something that you have promised you will do or you have to do.

To be committed means your willingness to work very hard at something.

In our context, it means that you are willing to work hard in serving God and making sure His Kingdom is advancing. You have promised to serve God, behave in a manner that will bring glory to God and His Kingdom, according to Kingdom principles. You have promised and are willing to do things God's way. You will no longer serve God in your way or on your own terms. You will serve God, when it is convenient and when it is not. This will bring the desired blessings and breakthroughs.

An example of commitment at its peak is found in the scripture below:

> *Now three of the thirty captains went down to the rock to David, into the cave of Adullam ; and the host of the Philistines encamped in the valley of Rephaim.*
>
> *And David was then in the hold, and the Philistines' garrison was then at Bethlehem.*
>
> *And David longed, and said, Oh that one would give me drink of the water of the well of Bethlehem that is at the gate.*
>
> *And the three brake through the host of the Philistines, and drew water out of the well of Bethlehem, that was by the gate, and took it, and brought it to David: but David would not drink of it, but poured it out to the Lord, and said, My God forbid it me, that I should do this thing: shall I drink the blood of these men that have put their lives in jeopardy? For with the jeopardy of their lives they brought it: therefore he would not drink it. These things did these three mightiest.*

1 Chronicles 11:15-19

From the above scripture, we can see the desire of the king; he desired to drink water from the well of Bethlehem. The bible says that the garrison of their enemy was there, the risk involved in satisfying the desire(the risk is to pass through the camp of the enemy before they can get water from the well of Bethlehem), the response of the committed(the three broke through the host of the Philistines), their return and the reward of their commitment.

There are other areas of commitment that we need to be involved in on our daily work in life. For us to see result or make progress in life we must be committed to the course or career we have been called into. We need to be committed to the following; We must be committed to self, committed to our family, career/job, committed to business, committed to personal development, committed to physical and spiritual fitness and committed to ministry. Our commitment should start from our commitment to God and this is the foundation in which other commitment should be built upon. But in this book I want to concentrate on commitment to God that brings testimony.

What is testimony?

According to Longman Dictionary of Contemporary English, testimony is a fact or situation that shows or proves very clearly that something exists or is true.

In this context, it shows or proves that God exist and He is true. How can you show or prove that God exist or He is true? You show or prove that God exist and He is true when you experience a miracle, success, breakthrough, healing, deliverance, prosperity, victory. These are the evidences that the gospel of Jesus is true and powerful. Because of outstanding evidences, people will want to come to serve your God. In Zechariah 8:23 the bible says, that, 'In those days ten men from every language of the nations shall grasp the sleeve of a Jewish man, saying, "Let us go with you, for we have heard *that* God *is* with you". This statement was made by God because of the promises of what He said He will do in the life of the Jews. The testimony and evidence of God's grace upon your life will make people to come to you and ask you to show them to your God.

God has promised us that we will not serve Him in vain. Our reward is not only waiting for us in heaven, but it is also here on earth. Hannah in 1 Samuel 1:26-27 shared a testimony that Samuel was the child she asked of the Lord and God granted her request. Samuel was the proof that God exists and He is true. Another great testimony is about Zacharias and Elizabeth in Luke 1: 5-14. The Bible says that Elizabeth was barren and both were well stricken in age. Because of the commitment of Zacharias to God which was demonstrated in his service to God, an angel visited him with good news. The good news or testimony was that Elizabeth will conceive and bear Zacharias a child at old age. Then in verse 57 and 58, the bible says that when Elizabeth's full time came for her to put to bed, she brought forth a son. It is not a coincidence that you are reading this right now; it has been ordained before the foundation of the world, so you will also share testimony in Jesus name. I will share some of my testimonies at the end of this book. God has rewarded my commitment to Him by giving me some outstanding testimonies in spite of the process that God is taking me through.

CHAPTER ONE

DEDICATE YOURSELF

For the promises of God to be fulfilled in your life, the first thing to do is to dedicate yourself to Him. Dedicating oneself requires total submission to God and His will and we find a perfect example in the Macedonian Church of the New Testament. The bible records concerning them that:

> *"Best of all, they went beyond our highest hopes, for their first action was to dedicate themselves to the Lord and to us, for whatever directions God might give to them through us."*
>
> **2 Corinthians 8:5(The Living Bible)**

Before any act of service whatsoever, the Macedonian Christians first dedicated themselves to God. Someone might then ask, "How can I dedicate myself to God practically?"
We find the answer in **2 Corinthians 6: 14 – 18**:

"Do not be unequally yoked together with unbelievers. For what fellowship has righteousness with lawlessness? And what communion has light with darkness? [15] And what accord has Christ with Belial? Or what part has a believer with an unbeliever? [16] And what agreement has the temple of God with idols? For you are the

temples of the living God. As God has said:"I will dwell in them And walk among them. I will be their God, and they shall be My people."

[17] Therefore "Come out from among them and be separate, says the Lord. Do not touch what is unclean, and I will receive you."[18] "I will be a Father to you, and you shall be My sons and daughters, Says the LORD Almighty."

The bible admonishes us not to team up or form close alliances with unbelievers, especially in the area of marriage. We ought to have no business with the works of darkness because we are the light of the world. There should be no harmony between us, who are the temple of God, and idols. As the temple of the living God, we have to be careful what we do with our body, minding the totality of our lifestyle. We cannot afford to live anyhow. When we do these, then God promises to live and work in us. He said He will be our God and Father. It is our duty to separate ourselves from whatsoever things that may defile us. Brethren, let us shun evil so that God can fulfill His great promises in and through us.

In **Gen.12:1**, the bible records,

"Now the LORD had said to Abram: "Get out of your country, From your family, And from your father's house, To a land that I will show you."

Abraham obeyed God by separating himself from his family, his country and his father's house. Until he did that, God could not bless him. The promises of God could not be fulfilled. There are certain people you must separate yourself from. There are some places you frequently go, that you need to stop going, in order to be fully dedicated to God.

Apostle James says that if you are a friend to the world, it will be impossible to be God's friend (James4:4). When you copy the pattern of this world, you cannot be a friend to God. Jesus told us in John 17:16 that though we are still living in this world, we are not **of** this world. We are resident here on earth but we are of heaven, so we should behave like children of the heavenly Kingdom. Our lives should bring glory to God.

In whatever field of endeavor you are, let your life and character bring glory to God. Let your light so shine among men that God will be glorified.

The World vs the World

In 1 John 2:15 – 17, the bible enjoins us:

"Do not love the world or anything in the world. If anyone loves the world, love for the Father is not in them. ¹⁶ For everything in the world—***the lust of the flesh, the lust of the eyes, and the pride of life***—comes not from the Father but from the world. ¹⁷ The world and its desires pass away, but whoever does the will of God lives forever."

It encourages us not to love the world or the things in it. If we love the world, it means the love of the Father is not in us. According to the above scripture everything we see in the physical world can be classified into three, namely:

- The lust of the flesh
- The lust of the eyes
- The pride of life

Let me differentiate between the world as used in 1 John 2:15 and the world as written in the popular John 3:16, "For God so loved the world that He gave His only begotten son....."

In John 3:16, the Bible lets us know that it was because of God's great love that He sent His only begotten Son to die for the world. Then in 1 John 2:15, the Bible tells us not to love the world. Is this a contradiction? What is the Bible saying here? The world in John 3:16 refers to the people or human beings in the world (God loves all the people on earth because He created them; they are His creation).However, the world as it is used in 1 John 2:15, is talking about the systems and patterns of operation in the world.

Overcoming Temptation

In Gen. 3:1-6, we find account of the first temptation. Satan tempted and deceived Eve in the Garden of Eden and much in the same manner, that evil serpent came and tempted Jesus in the wilderness, after 40 days' fast (Mt. 4:1-11). In Gen. 3:6, the bible narrates, "*And when the woman saw that the tree was **good for food,** and that it was **pleasant to the eyes**, and a tree to be desired **to make one wise**, she took of the fruit thereof, and did eat, and gave also unto her husband with her; and he did eat.*"
Eve saw that the tree was:

a.)   Good for food, which represents lust of the flesh

b.)   Pleasant to the eyes signifies lust of the eyes and ;

c.)   To be desired to make one wise, points to the pride of life.

A study of the temptations of Jesus shows us something similar.
1. Matt.4:3 – In the first temptation, the devil asked Jesus to turn stones to bread pointing to lust of the flesh. In verses 5 – 6, he asked him to throw Himself down from a height, in order to prove his Sonship as God's son. This is representative of the pride of life. Unfortunately, many today fail this test as they are proud because of what possessions and positions they are privileged to have. Finally, Satan, in verses 8 and 9, showed Jesus the kingdoms of the world and the beauty attached to them, and then asked him to bow and worship him. He promised to give Jesus all those kingdoms He could see – the lust of the eyes.

While Eve fell to temptation, Jesus was able to overcome by the Word of God. Today, the pattern has not changed - the devil is tempting believers every moment, hoping they will fall as Eve did. Now, we find people commit different atrocities because of the luxuries they desire, wanting to get them by all means. The devil has no different operating tactics – it has been the same, right from the Garden of Eden. He is a master in the realm of the flesh. The devil has been studying the flesh for about six thousand years. The only way to defeat him is in the realm of the spirit, the way Jesus defeated him.

The bible in Galatians 5:16tells us to: ***"Walk in the Spirit, and you will not fulfill the lust of the flesh"***.

When you have the love of the world in your heart, you will easily fall prey to the devil's temptations. Once the devil sees that your heart is set on the things of the world, he will quickly come to help you fulfill those carnal desires, with the ultimate aim to steal, kill and destroy your God given blessings(John 10:10). That will not be your portion in Jesus name.

Sadly, some people's belly is their god. Mere food has made many to fall into the hands of the enemy. There are some who once they see anything beautiful and dazzling, will want to get it by all means (legal or not). Some men are so filled with lust that they cannot turn their eyes away from any woman that passes by. The same applies to some women.1 Jn. 2:15-17

To love God is to be a friend to God (James 4:4). God will be our Father (2 Cor. 6:17 -18) as we make the decision to obey Him. As we believers face temptations every day, we must ask God for strength to overcome the devil every moment. Let us give no room for him to rob us of God's blessings in our lives.

What God Hates

Dedication to God also means that we hate what God hates and obey His commandments. What are the things God hates? Let's look at them in **Proverbs 6: 16-19:**

"These six things the LORD hates, Yes, seven are an abomination to Him: A proud look, A lying tongue, Hands that shed innocent blood,

A heart that devises wicked plans, Feet that are swift in running to evil; A false witness who speaks lies, And one who sows discord among brethren."

1. A Proud Look(Pride)

What is pride? The Longman Dictionary of Contemporary English defines pride as belief that you are better than other people and do not need their help or support. Mounce's Complete Expository Dictionary of Old and New Testament Words defines a proud person as someone that is boastful - somebody that glories in himself or herself.

Another word that is similar to this is arrogance, which means someone behaving in a rude way, because they think they are very important. An arrogant person will always have an unteachable spirit and God resists such people. If you do not want God to resist you, learn to be teachable.

James 4:6 says that God resists the proud, but gives grace to the humble. God detests the proud.

Pride brought Satan down, when he became arrogant and boastful. He overestimated himself and wanted to be like God. So if we are boastful and keep overestimating ourselves, we may fall into the same situation that Satan found himself **Isa.14:12-15**

What will happen to the proud? God will not endure him.

"Whoever secretly slanders his neighbor, him I will destroy; The one who has a haughty look and a proud heart, him I will not endure." - **Psalm 101:5**

"Look on everyone who is proud, and bring him low; tread down the wicked in their place.

Hide them in the dust together, bind their faces in hidden darkness."

-   ***Job 40:12-13***

"Now I, Nebuchadnezzar, praise and extol and honor the King of heaven, all of whose works are truth, and His ways justice. And those who walk in pride He is able to put down."

-   **Daniel 4:37**

"But when his heart was lifted up, and his spirit was hardened in pride, he was deposed from his kingly throne, and they took his glory from him."

-   ***Daniel 5:20***

When men's hearts are lifted and hardened in pride, no amount of advice given to them can convince them about anything. The outcome is often that they lose their positions and glory.

An example of a proud person is found in **Acts 12:20-23:**

> *"Now Herod had been very angry with the people of Tyre and Sidon; but they came to him with one accord, and having made Blastus the king's personal aide their friend, they asked for peace, because their country was supplied with food by the king's country. So on a set day Herod, arrayed in royal apparel, sat on his throne and gave an oration to them. And the people kept shouting, "The voice of a god and not of a man". Then immediately an angel of the Lord struck him, because he did not give glory to God. And he was eaten by worms and died."*

King Herod grew proud because of his power and influence since he supplied food to other nations, which paid allegiance to him. Instead of giving glory to God, he let the fame get into his head and unfortunately suffered destruction.

So brethren, are you proud today because you have some money in your bank account and you have the ability to give assistance to others? Is your education making you proud and arrogant? Or is it because of the influential position you are occupying?

Examine yourself to see if there is any trace of pride in you so that you can repent immediately. The Bible says pride comes before a fall. All you have today has been given to you by God. All you are today, God made you. It is God that has lifted you out of poverty and placed you among kings. Give Him the glory for it.

My prayer for you is that you will not fall like Herod in Jesus Name.

2.   A lying tongue

"But the cowardly, unbelieving, abominable, murderers, sexually immoral, sorcerers, idolaters, and all liars shall have their part in the lake which burns with fire and brimstone, which is the second death."

-   **Revelation 21:8**

It is very clear here what will happen to liars. There is nothing like small or big lie. No matter the degree of lie, the punishment is the lake of fire. I implore you to as much as possible, avoid compromising situations. The Bible says that our yes should be yes and our no, no. See what happened to Ananias and Sapphira in Acts 5:1-10:

But a certain man named Ananias, with Sapphira his wife, sold a possession. ² And he kept back part of the proceeds, his wife also being aware of it, and brought a certain part and laid it at the apostles' feet. ³ But Peter said, "Ananias, why has Satan filled your heart to lie to the Holy Spirit and keep back part of the price of the land for yourself? ⁴ While it remained, was it not your own? And after it was sold, was it not in your own control? Why have you conceived this thing in your heart? You have not lied to men but to God."

⁵ Then Ananias, hearing these words, fell down and breathed his last. So great fear came upon all those who heard these things. ⁶ And the young men arose and wrapped him up, carried him out, and buried him. ⁷ Now it was about three hours later when his wife came in, not knowing what had happened. ⁸ And Peter answered her, "Tell me whether you sold the land for so much?" She said, "Yes, for so much." Then Peter said to her, "How is it that you have agreed together to test the Spirit of the Lord? Look, the feet of those who have buried your husband are at the door, and they will carry you out." ¹⁰ Then immediately she fell down at his feet and breathed her last. And the young men came in and found her dead, and carrying her out, buried her by her husband.

This man and his wife connived together to lie to the Apostles concerning the sale of their property. Many were surprised at what happened because the said property belonged to them. They had the right to give out the money or not, but because they lied and did not bring all the proceeds, they died instantly.

3. Hands that shed innocent blood.

"When you spread out your hands, I will hide My eyes from you; Even though you make many prayers, I will not hear. Your hands are full of blood. Wash yourselves, make yourselves clean; put away the evil of your doings from before My eyes. Cease to do evil."

-   **Isaiah 1:15-16**

Here, God was rebuking the people for their evil deeds. He said because of these evils, when the people spread their hands in prayer (worship), He would not hear them. Can you see why some people's prayers are not answered? Shedding of innocent blood can be by done through killing e.g. murder, human rituals and sacrifice, abortion, rape a virgin and spill her blood, witchcraft that eat and drink people's blood etc.

The blood of those that was shed cry to God for vengeance. "And the Lord said unto Cain, Where is Abel thy brother? And he said, I know not: Am I my brother's keeper? And he said, What hast thou done? the voice of thy brother's blood crieth unto me from the ground." Genesis 4:9-10

"And when he had opened the fifth seal, I saw under the altar the souls of them that were slain for the word of God, and for the testimony which they held: And they cried with a loud voice, saying, How long, O Lord, holy and true, dost thou not judge and avenge our blood on them that dwell on the earth?" Revelation 6:9-10

Anyone who has a past of shedding innocent blood, one way or the other and has not taken time to pray for God's mercy needs to do so as soon as possible. Pray that the blood of Jesus will silence every blood crying against your life, in the name of Jesus. Pray that
 every crying blood of your father's house be silenced, in the name of Jesus. It is expedient, because without it prayers are hindered. And after receiving God's mercy, such a person should desist from it.

4. A heart that devises wicked plans

> **"Then the Lord saw that the wickedness of man was great in the earth, and that every intent of the thoughts of his heart was only evil continually."**
>
> **-   Genesis 6:5**

What were the things that God saw on the earth that made Him to be sorry for creating man? He saw wickedness, corruption and violence. The sons of God were marrying the daughters of men (unequal yoking with unbelievers). Paul gave a good description of this in **Romans 1:21**: *"Because, although they knew God, they did not glorify Him as God, nor were thankful, but became futile in their thoughts, and their foolish hearts were darkened. Professing to be wise, they became fools, and changed the glory of the incorruptible God into an image made like corruptible man- and birds and four-footed animals and creeping things...."*

The things they were involved in made God sorry for creating man. Everyone needs to check themselves and see if there is any area that needs amendment, and repent to avert the wrath of God.

"The heart is deceitful above all things, and desperately wicked; Who can know it? I, the Lord, search the heart, I test the mind, Even to give every man according to the fruit of his doings."

- ***Jeremiah 17:9-10***

So if the Lord were to search your heart, what will He find? Is it wickedness and deception or good thoughts? Maybe what you have now is what you deserve based on the state of your heart. You need to begin to renew your mind according to the word of God.

5. Feet that are swift in running to evil

> **"All have turned away; they have together become worthless; there is no one who does good, not even one. Their throats are open graves; their tongues practice deceit. The poison of vipers is on their lips. Their mouths are full of cursing and bitterness. "Their feet are swift to shed blood; ruin and misery mark their ways, and the way of peace they do not know. There is no fear of God before their eyes."**

- Romans 3:12-18

The Lord does not approve of people, who are quick and delight to be involved in immoral and criminal behaviors. Yet we find quite a number of professing Christians falling into this category.

6. A False witness

[7] Then Jezebel his wife said to him, "You now exercise authority over Israel! Arise, eat food, and let your heart be cheerful; I will give you the vineyard of Naboth the Jezreelite."[8] And she wrote letters in Ahab's name, sealed them with his seal, and sent the letters to the elders and the nobles who were dwelling in the city with Naboth. [9] She wrote in the letters, saying, Proclaim a fast, and seat Naboth with high honor among the people; [10] and seat two men, scoundrels, before him to bear witness against him, saying, "You have blasphemed God and the king." Then take him out, and stone him, that he may die.[1] So the men of his city, the elders and nobles who were inhabitants of his city, did as Jezebel had sent to them, as it was written in the letters which she had sent to them. [12] They proclaimed a fast, and seated Naboth with high honor among the people. [13] And two men, scoundrels, came in and sat before him; and the scoundrels witnessed against him, against Naboth, in the presence of the people, saying, "Naboth has blasphemed God and the king!" Then they took him outside the city and stoned him with stones, so that he died. [14] Then they sent to Jezebel, saying, "Naboth has been stoned and is dead."

[15] And it came to pass, when Jezebel heard that Naboth had been stoned and was dead, that Jezebel said to Ahab, "Arise,

*take possession of the vineyard of Naboth the Jezreelite,
which he refused to give you for money; for Naboth is not
alive, but dead." ¹⁶ So it was, when Ahab heard that Naboth
was dead, that Ahab got up and went down to take
possession of the vineyard of Naboth the Jezreelite.*

The LORD Condemns Ahab

*¹⁷ Then the word of the LORD came to Elijah the Tishbite,
saying, ¹⁸ "Arise, go down to meet Ahab king of Israel, who
lives in Samaria. There he is, in the vineyard of Naboth, where
he has gone down to take possession of it. ¹⁹ You shall speak
to him, saying, 'Thus says the LORD: "Have you murdered and
also taken possession?"' And you shall speak to him, saying,
'Thus says the LORD: "In the place where dogs licked the
blood of Naboth, dogs shall lick your blood, even yours."'"*

²⁰ So Ahab said to Elijah, "Have you found me, O my enemy?"

*And he answered, "I have found you, because you have sold
yourself to do evil in the sight of the LORD: ²¹ 'Behold, I will
bring calamity on you. I will take away your posterity, and will
cut off from Ahab every male in Israel, both bond and free. ²² I
will make your house like the house of Jeroboam the son of
Nebat, and like the house of Baasha the son of Ahijah,
because of the provocation with which you have provoked Me
to anger, and made Israel sin.' ²³ And concerning Jezebel the
LORD also spoke, saying, 'The dogs shall eat Jezebel by the
wall of Jezreel.' ²⁴ The dogs shall eat whoever belongs to
Ahab and dies in the city, and the birds of the air shall eat
whoever dies in the field."*

Jezebel planned for false witnesses to lie against Naboth so she could forcefully inherit his property. She succeeded but lost her life in the end because God took vengeance for that poor man.

7) He that sows discord

Psalm 27:12

> *Do not deliver me to the will of my adversaries;*
> *For false witnesses have risen against me,*
> *And such as breathe out violence.*

God hates divorce

"And this have ye done again, covering the altar of the LORD with tears, with weeping, and with crying out, insomuch that he regarded not the offering any more, or receives it with good will at your hand. Yet ye say, wherefore? Because the LORD hath been witness between thee and the wife of thy youth, against whom thou hast dealt treacherously: yet is she thy companion, and the wife of thy covenant. And did not he make one?

Yet had he the residue of the spirit. And wherefore one? That he might seek a godly seed. Therefore take heed to your spirit, and let none deal treacherously against the wife of his youth. For the LORD, the God of Israel, saith that he hates putting away: for one covered violence with his garment, saith the LORD of hosts: therefore take heed to your spirit, that ye deal not treacherously."

- **Malachi 2:13-16**

The Lord hates divorce. At this juncture, I will advise single brothers and sisters, please, when choosing your life partner, make sure that it is the person the Lord desires you to marry because once married, there is no going back. You have to be faithful to your wife because the Lord will be witness at the marriage. Your vow on the wedding day binds you to be faithful and loyal to your spouse, as long as you live.

Many are suffering today in business and many areas of their lives because of unfaithfulness to their spouse. For the married ones, who have not been faithful to their spouses, please pause for a minute, repent and ask God for mercy. Then make a personal decision to remain faithful to your spouse.

Conclusion

To dedicate yourself to God means to live in a way that pleases Him and shun evil in all ramifications.

If you find out that you fall short in anyway, there is room for repentance. This is the first step to take to receive salvation (restoration) that God offers to us in the Lord Jesus Christ. Acts 2:36-38, Acts 17:30

True repentance is sorrow toward God. Psalms 51:1-4

It is also being truthful about your sin. Psalms 32:5

It is turning away from your sin. Proverb 28:13, Zechariah 1:3-4

You must also turn from yourself. 2 Corinthians 5:15

When there is true repentance, there is always restoration.

CHAPTER 2

STUDY THE WORD

Necessity is laid upon every believer in Christ to know and have in-depth understanding of God's Word. You have to know God for yourself and this is only possible through reading, studying and meditating on His Word. In Isaiah 43:10, God said we have been chosen to know Him.

John 1:1 tells us that:

"In the beginning was the Word, and the Word was with God and the Word was God."

This bible verse establishes that God is the same as His word. If God is His word, then you have to know the Word in order to know God well. Once you know God, His Word will bring success and prosperity.

Who is God?

1) God is the Creator of everything. He created the heavens and the earth. He created visible and invisible things. There is nothing that exists today that was not made by God. Neh. 9:6

2) God is all-powerful. 1 Chronicles 29:11, Ephesians 3:20

3) God is all-knowing. 1 John 3:20, Hebrews 4:13

4) God is Holy. 1 Samuel 2:2

5) God is a Spirit. John 4:24

6) God is a loving Father. 1 John 3:1

Who are we to God?

1) Created by God. Psalms 139:14-16

2) Owned by God. 1 Corinthians 6:19-20

3) Called to worship God. Revelation 4:11

The Origin of the Word (The Bible)

How did the Word of God come about? Who wrote it? The bible itself gives us the answer to these questions. Apostle Peter wrote along that line in one of his epistles thus:

"Knowing this first, that no prophecy of the scripture is of any private interpretation. For the prophecy came not in old time by the will of man: but holy men of God spake as they were moved by the Holy Ghost."

- **2Pet.1:20-21**

In one of his letters to Timothy, Apostle Paul also gives us insight into the purpose for which the bible was written. He writes:

"All scripture is given by inspiration of God, and is profitable for doctrine, for reproof, for correction, for instruction in righteousness."

- **2Tim.3:16**

By these scriptures we know that the Word of God came from God. It was by inspiration that the men of old spoke and wrote what is today called the Bible. They wrote as the Holy Spirit inspired and led them to. The Word of God did not come by the will of man.

What does it mean to study the Word?

The Bible says in **2 Timothy 2:15**:

"Study to show yourself approved unto God, a workman that needed not to be ashamed, rightly dividing the word of truth."

God's desire for us is to study so that we can get His approval. That means if you do not study, you will not be approved by God.

The Longman, Dictionary of Contemporary English gives the following definition of study:

When you spend time learning, especially at home or by yourself rather than during school.

The key word here is **spending time**. You have to make a quality decision to set time aside to do this. This is where your commitment is needed. The principle is continuity. You cannot afford to start today, do it for a week or two and then stop. No! It has to be continuous for you to have a testimony.

Knowledge is very important. You have to seek for it as you seek for silver and gold.

"Now I say, That the heir, as long as he is a child, differeth nothing from a servant, though he be lord of all; But is under tutors and governors until the time appointed of the father. Even so we, when we were children, were in bondage under the elements of the world. But when the fullness of the time was come, God sent forth his Son, made of a woman, made under the law, To redeem them that were under the law, that we might receive the adoption of sons."

- **Galatians 4:1-5**

In the Galatians scriptures above, the bible lets us know that we are sons, with inheritances in God's Kingdom, but we will not be any different from slaves if we don't study to find out the things that are rightfully ours.

Why Study The Bible?

1) The Bible is the only source of complete revelation of God and the plan of God for man.

2) The Word of God can guide and discipline you. 2 Timothy 3:16-17

3) The Word of God is your weapon for spiritual warfare. Ephesians 6:17

4) It reveals to you your inheritance as a believer. Acts 20: 32

5) It gives you encouragement and hope Romans.15:4

6) It gives you confidence to share the gospel. 1 Peter 3:15

7) The word of God with the help of the Holy Spirit has the ability to transform your habits and characters. 2 Corinthians 3:18. It is the power of the Holy Spirit working through the word of God that brings victories into your life.

In addition, here are some very important scriptures about the necessity of being acquitted with the Word of God:

1. *"This book of the law shall not depart out of thy mouth, but thou shall meditate in it day and night, and observe all that is written therein, whereby thou shalt make thy way prosperous and have good success."*

- **Joshua 1:8**

For Joshua to succeed in life and ministry, he had to follow these instructions. The word of God was:

a. Not to depart from his mouth. He had to speak the word all the time.

b. Meditate on the word of God every moment of his life

c. Observe and do the word.

After these instructions, came the promise. His obedience to the instructions made his ways prosperous and enabled him to have good success.

Our success and prosperity depend on obedience to divine instructions. The ball lies in our court. We are responsible for our success or failure, prosperity or poverty. If we are not succeeding or prospering, it is not God's fault. I am glad that my success and prosperity does not depend on anyone. Since I discovered this, I study the Word seriously and have been sowing it for years now.

If you also want to succeed and prosper, you have to decide to start sowing the seed of God's Word into your spirit.

2. *"Blessed is the man that walked not in the counsel of the ungodly, nor standeth in the way of sinners, nor sitteth in the seat of the scornful. But his delight is in the law of the LORD; and in his law doth he meditate day and night. And he shall be like a tree planted by the rivers of water, that bringeth forth his fruit in his season; his leaf also shall not wither; and whatsoever he doeth shall prosper)."*

- Psalm 1:1-3

Who is the man that desires blessings from God? He should not follow the advice of evil men or hang around sinners. He should not sit where people are scoffing at the things of God. He is someone who delights in the Word of God and meditates on it at every given opportunity - day and night.

Anyone who does these is likened to a tree planted by the river side – which never experiences drought. Its leaves never wither. Instead, it produces fruit all year long. Likewise, you will always prosper in whatever you do when you fear God.

3. **Prov. 4:20-22**

It is our responsibility to give attention to the word of God - incline our ears to the sayings of God and not allow it to depart from before our memory. With these done, it is guaranteed that the word of God will bring health to your flesh. It will bring life to you - not just life but abundant life.

Do you desire health or healing? Go for the Word. Do you desire a life of peace, success and prosperity? Go for the Word.

4. *"And now, brethren, I commend you to God, and to the word of his grace, which is able to build you up, and to give you an inheritance among all them which are sanctified."*

- Acts 20:32

The Word of God (Word of His grace) has the ability to build you up (character wise, spiritually, materially, financially, etc.) and it also has the ability to give you inheritance (All that the heavenly Father has given to you in his **will**). The word of God is the will of God. Study this **WILL** so that you will not suffer from ignorance. As we grow spiritually, we easily get all that the Father has in store for us(Gal. 4:1-2)

5. *"Let the word of Christ dwell in you richly in all wisdom; teaching and admonishing one another in psalms and hymns and spiritual songs, singing with grace in your hearts to the Lord."*

-   Col. 3:16

It is our responsibility to let the Word of Christ dwell in us richly. We have to make effort to put it there, to deposit it in our hearts like cash in a bank account. When it dwells in you richly, it will be in all wisdom and you will be able to apply the word to your situation. Also, you will be able to teach and admonish others. No deposit, no returns.

Brothers and sisters, from the above five scriptures, it is obvious that each individual has a role to play in their being prosperous and successful in life.

Benefits of the Word

- The Word is an unshakable foundation for life and ministry.

Let whatever you want to do have a root from the word of God. Your foundation in the Word will determine your strength and height in life. Live by the word.

> *"But He answered and said," It is written,' Man shall not live by bread alone, but by every word that proceeds from the mouth of God."-* **Matthew 4:4**

*"Whosoever cometh to me, and heareth my sayings, and doeth them, I will shew you to whom he is like. He is like a man which built an house, and digged deep, and laid the foundation on a rock: and when the flood arose, the stream beat vehemently upon that house, and could not shake it: for it was founded upon a rock".***Luke 6:47-48**

- The Word of God has the power to cleanse.

"Wherewithal shall a young man cleanse his way? By taking heed thereto according to thy word." **Psalm 119:9**

- The Word of God has the power and ability to keep one from sin.

*"Thy word have I hid in mine heart, that I might not sin against thee."***Psalm 119:11**

- The Word of God has the power to give hope, comfort and life.

*"Remember the word unto thy servant, upon which thou hast caused me to hope.   This is my comfort in my affliction: for thy word hath quickened me."***Psalm 119:49-50**

- There is assurance in the Word of God. The blessings are settled in heaven.

"Forever, O LORD, thy word is settled in heaven." **Psalm 119:89**

- The Word of God gives direction and guidance.

"Thy word is a lamp unto my feet, and a light unto my path." **Psalm 119:105**

"The entrance of thy word giveth light; it giveth understanding unto the simple." **Ps. 119:130**

- There are great treasures in the Word of God.

"I rejoice at thy word, as one that findeth great spoil." **Psalm 119:16**

Portraits of the Word in Scriptures

1) The Word of God is like water, it has the ability to cleanse you and keep you clean. John 15:3 and Ephesians 5:25-27

2) The Word of God is a seed. When you plant seed it germinates and bear fruits. When you sow the Word of God in your heart, it has the ability to grow and bear fruits in your life. Luke 8:11

3) The Word of God is like a sword. It has the ability to pierce through every hard situation. Ephesians 6:17 and Hebrews 4:12

4) The Word of God is like Lamp and light. It gives direction and can shine in every dark part of your life. Psalm 119:105 and 2Peter 1:19

5) The Word of God is like rain that produces fruit. Isaiah 55:10

6) The Word of God is like a destroying hammer. It has the ability to destroy every hard situation in your life. Jeremiah 23:29

How to Use the Word

The heart to mouth principle (Romans 10:6-10)

The Word of God must first enter your heart, which is why when the Word is being preached or taught, you have to open your heart to receive. Your heart is the soil on which the Word will germinate (Luke 8:15). When it is in abundance in your heart, it will begin to come out. Jesus Christ said that out of the abundance of the heart the mouth speaks (Luke 6:45).

Once you begin to declare the Word with your mouth, the Word will produce fruits(Mark 11:22-23). Because you are a king, your command will be backed with spiritual power (Ecclesiastes 8:4). Whatever you say at this time by faith will always come to pass.

When engaging in a spiritual battle, it is important to declare to declare the Word of God. This is how to get salvation and deliverance. A Spiritual battle differs from a physical one, so you don't need physical weapons and techniques to win the battle. In the spirit realm, what works are words.

You are not fighting against people with flesh and blood, but against spirits without bodies. Physical demonstrations during prayers do not have any impact on those spiritual beings. These evil and satanic rulers are unseen which cannot be touched or dealt with by combat styles. The ONLY THING that affects and disempowers them is the WORD OF GOD. They respond to the spoken Word which is declared during prayer.

You must declare these words with authority and when it is God's Word it will be accomplished with power. This is what defeats them. Empty words, that is, your own words, cannot do the job. It is God's Word that you have stored in your heart which is now in abundance that guarantees victory.

How to Study the Bible

Your approach to God's Word is very important. When you decide to study, you must be consistent. You must keep your word. This is integrity. Your consistency shows your seriousness.

However, this is easier done when you can establish a particular convenient time to study. This time could either be during the day or at night. Just ensure that it is a period when there are no distractions so you can have full concentration.

You should also have a good place to study and a good atmosphere.

Before studying, pray the prayer of Apostle Paul as contained in Eph.1:16-17. (That God will give you the spirit of wisdom and revelation and that your eyes of understanding will be enlightened)

Someone might ask, Pastor how can I study my bible, when I don't even understand what I read most of the time?

James gave us a very simple and easy way to do it.

"Wherefore lay apart all filthiness and superfluity of naughtiness, and receive with meekness the engrafted word, which is able to save your souls. But be ye doers of the word, and not hearers only, deceiving your own selves. For if any be a hearer of the word, and not a doer, he is like unto a man beholding his natural face in a glass: For he beholdeth himself, and goeth his way, and straightway forgetteth what manner of man he was.

But whoso looketh into the perfect law of liberty, and continueth therein, he being not a forgetful hearer, but a doer of the work, this man shall be blessed in his deed." **James 1:21-25**

Firstly, begin your study with an open heart to receive from God as you read His Word. Read and study with the mind that God will speak to you through the Word you are reading. Do not read with sentiments or with your experience because God's word is new every day.

Read with a mind willing to obey whatever instructions the word is going to give you. It is one thing to read or hear God's word; it is another thing for you to obey.

So as not to be a forgetful hearer, you have to read on a daily basis. Whether you understand it or not, continue to read on a daily basis. You can ask questions during the bible study class in your church about those scripture passages you do not understand. Continuous reading will help you not to be a forgetful hearer but a doer of the Word. This is what will bring the blessings.

Tools for Bible Study

1) The Holy Bible. For you to have a good and in-depth study, you should have at least five different versions of the Bible (The King James Version, New King James Version, New International Version, Amplified Version, and New Living Translation).

2) Bible Concordance

3) Bible Dictionary

4) Notebook and pen

5) Bible Commentary

6) Other writings(Books)

Methods of Study

1) **Character Study**: Here, you focus on a character or personality from the Bible. E.g. Apostle Paul. Search your bible for every place where Paul was mentioned.

PAUL: His background

He was originally called Saul and he is from Tarsus - *"And the Lord said unto him, Arise, and go into the street which is called Straight, and enquire in the house of Judas for one called Saul, of Tarsus: for, behold, he prayeth."***Acts 9:11**

He was from the tribe of Benjamin, a Pharisee **Phil. 3:5**
He was educated by Gamaliel **Acts 22:3**
He was unmarried**1 Cor. 7:8**

His Life as a Persecutor

He assisted in the stoning of Stephen**Acts7:58**

He zealously persecuted the Church **Acts9:1-2**

His Life as an Apostle

He was called as a missionary to the Gentiles. He went to Arabia, preached in Damascus and escaped in a basket.

His first missionary journey- acts 13:2-4

His second missionary journey- acts 15:36-41

His third missionary journey- acts 19:1-22

Significant Issues in His Writings

1) His Apostleship **1 Corinthians 9:1-3**

2) Salvation possible only in the name of Jesus **Romans 3:21-26**

3) Salvation through faith alone **Galatians 2:15-21**

4) Circumcision not necessary for salvation **Romans 4:9-12**

5) Christian freedom **1 Corinthians 8:1-13**

6) Proper use of spiritual gifts**1 Corinthians 12:1-14**

7) Life led by the Spirit of God **Romans 8:1-17**

8) Proper order in the Church**1 Corinthians 11:17-34**

Study Application

How have you been affected by studying the life of Paul? His life showed that of a man who really walked with God, knew his purpose and fulfilled that purpose.

Your application would then mean that you can make a quality decision to walk with God, discover your purpose and fulfill that purpose. You have to pray to God to reveal your purpose to you (if you don't know it yet) and grace to walk in that purpose in order to positively influence your generation.

2) **Verse by verse Study**: Here, you pick a verse and look for all the references in the Bible concerning that particular verse. For example Romans 1:17, pick a concept or word and list everything that is said about the word or phrase. Then pick a concordance to look for that word or phrase in other scriptures. Habakkuk 2:4, Romans1:17, Hebrews 10:38, Galatians 3:11. Look for examples of those that have lived by faith. One example that comes to mind is Abraham. The Bible says in **Hebrews 11:8-10:**

"By faith Abraham, when he was called to go out to a place which he would after receive for an inheritance, obeyed; and he went out, not knowing whither he went. By faith he sojourned in the land of promise, as in a strange country, dwelling in tabernacles with Isaac and Jacob, the heirs with him of the same promise: For he looked for a city which hath foundations, whose builder and maker is God."

Then in Romans **4:16-21**:

"Therefore <u>it is of faith</u>, that it might be by grace; to the end the promise might be sure to all the seed; not to that only which is of the law, but to that also which is of the <u>faith of Abraham</u>; who is the father of us all, (As it is written, I have made thee a father of many nations,) before him whom he believed, even God, who quickened the dead, and calleth those things which be not as though they were.

<u>Who against hope believed in hope</u>, that he might become the father of many nations, according to that which was spoken, So shall thy seed be. <u>And being not weak in faith</u>, he considered not his own body now dead, when he was about an hundred years old, neither yet the deadness of Sarah's womb: He staggered not at the promise of God through unbelief; but was <u>strong in faith</u>, giving glory to God; And being fully persuaded that, what he had promised, he was able also to perform."

These scriptures describe Abraham as a man of faith. He believed and trusted God, which was why he left his father's house, his country and kindred to a land he did not even know. He believed God to the extent of not doubting the promise of a son in his old age. The Bible says he hoped against hope. He was not weak in faith and he was strong in faith.

Study Application

How can you apply this to your life and situation?

For you to walk with God you must have faith in God. You must believe and trust God for what He has said to you. It may look foolish, but you must trust and obey. You must not be weak in faith, because there will come a time when it seems that what God has promised will not come to pass. You must be strong in faith and hold on to the word of God concerning that issue. Then you need to pray along this so that in every situation you would be able to walk in faith as Abraham walked with God in faith.

3) **Topical Study:** In this method, you pick a topic that you desire to study. Then you check its meaning in the dictionary. After that, you begin to look for everything that the bible has to say on the topic. Here are some topics you can do a study on: Covenant, Redemption, Reconciliation, Baptism, Sin, Grace, Atonement, Holiness, Confession, God, Heart, Heaven, and many others. Let us take Covenant as a case study.

Look for the meaning of **Covenant**: An agreement established between two people or parties. Covenant can be between humans and it can also be between man and God.

Let us look at some **covenants between humans** in the Bible.

Between Isaac and Abimelech - Genesis 26:26-31

Between Jacob and Laban - Genesis 31-43-54

Between Joshua and the Gibeonites - Joshua 9:3-15

Between David and Jonathan - 1 Samuel 18:3

Between Joash and the people - 2 kings 11:17

Between Zedekiah and the people - Jeremiah 34: 8-10

What are the elements in these covenants?

- Promises - 1 Samuel 20:14-17
- Stipulations - 2 Samuel 3:13
- Oaths - Genesis 31:53
- Responsibilities - 2Kings 12:8
- Witnesses - Genesis 31:45-48

Covenants between God and humans

- With Adam before the fall - Genesis 2:15-17
- With Noah - Genesis 9:1-19
- With Abram - Genesis 12:1-3
- With Israel at Sinai - Exodus 19:5-8
- With Israel before entering Palestine - Deut.29-30
- With Israel in the promise land - Joshua 24:1-27
- With David - 2 Samuel 7:14-17

- Future Covenant of peace - Ezekiel 34:25-31
- The New Covenant - Jeremiah 34:33-34

4) **Book Study**: This method gives you the opportunity to study each book of the Bible. Choose any book from the 66 books and do an in-depth study on the entire book. Find out the author, the date the book was written, the contents, the purpose of writing and the outline of the book. Let's use the book of Malachi as an example.

The author is Prophet Malachi

Date of writing is about 430B.C

Purpose of writing is to confront the people with their sin of insincere worship and corruption and to restore their relationship with God.

When you read the entire book, you will find the content (the main issues Prophet Malachi addressed).

Then you will need to apply it to yourself or your situation. How has this book affected you or spoken to you? In what areas do you need to amend your relationship with God? What lessons have you learnt? Make quality decision to walk according to what you have learnt. And finally, pray that God will give you the grace to abide and obey.

CHAPTER THREE

COMMUNION WITH GOD

After studying the Word (that is God talking to you through His Word), you have to communicate back to Him in prayer. Once you know His will (mind) after studying His word, take the Word (promises) and ask for whatever you want. It must line up with His will. If not asked according to His will, the prayers might not be answered.

14 And we are sure of this that he will listen to us whenever we ask him for anything in line with his will. 15 And if we really know he is listening when we talk to him and make our requests, then we can be sure that he will answer us.

- **1 John 5:14 -15**

Many people find it difficult to pray because they are unsure if God will hear and grant their petitions. John, the beloved, through the Holy Spirit assures us that we can have confidence in God, who listens to and answers prayers, when we ask anything in line with His will. This is the assurance of answered prayers. If you want to have this assurance, you have to know His will and ask accordingly. This is very important to you as a born again Christian.

When you pray out of His will, you pray amiss. When you pray out of a wrong motive, you cannot receive from God. Apostle James tells us that many believers struggle over nothing. They quarrel and fight one another because they are unable to get their desire due to envy and strife(James 4:1-3). For this reason, they engage in all sorts of shady deals to get their desires come pass. He goes on to say that the reason for this is that some believers do not ask God and even the ones that ask, do not get because they ask with wrong motives(only for pleasures).If you want your prayers to be answered speedily, ask according to the will and desire of heaven.

Persistence in Prayers

Furthermore, as a child of God, who desires to see results, you have to be persistent in prayers. To be persistent means to be determined to do something, even though it is difficult or other people oppose it. Persistence also means when something continues to exist or happen, especially for longer than is usual or desirable.

To be persistent in prayer is therefore to have the determination to continue to pray though it is sometimes difficult, and for a longer period than usual.

Continue to present your requests before God with determination even though it may have taken a long time. It is in your continuity that the answer will come. You don't have to give up because the answer has not come, it will surely come.

In Isaiah 62:6 -9, we are urged to pray until God's promises are fulfilled in our lives. It says we should not give God rest until we see the answer to our prayers. Our Lord Jesus told a story to buttress this point in one of his teachings on prayer. The bible records:

"Then teaching more about prayer, he used this illustration: suppose you went to a friend's house at midnight, wanting to borrow three loaves of bread. You would shout up to him, 'A friend of mine has just arrived for a visit and I've nothing to give him to eat.' He would call down from the bedroom, 'Please don't ask me to get up. The door is locked for the night and we are all in bed, I just can't help you this time.'

"But I will tell you this—though he won't do it as a friend, if you <u>keep knocking long enough</u> he will get up and give you everything you want—<u>just because of your persistence</u>. And so it is with prayer—keep on asking and you will keep on getting; keep on looking and you will keep on finding; knock and the door will be opened. Everyone who asks receives; all who seek, find; and the door is opened to everyone who knocks."

- **Luke 11:5-10**

Some Prayers of the Spirit

"Cease not to give thanks for you, making mention of you in my prayers; That the God of our Lord Jesus Christ, the Father of glory, <u>may give unto you the spirit of wisdom and revelation in the knowledge of him</u>: <u>The eyes of your understanding being enlightened</u>; that ye may know what is the hope of his calling, and what the riches of the glory of his inheritance in the saints."

Ephesians 1:16-18

"For this cause I bow my knees unto the Father of our Lord Jesus Christ, Of whom the whole family in heaven and earth is named, That he would grant you, according to the riches of his glory, <u>to be strengthened with might by his Spirit in the inner man</u>; That Christ may dwell in your hearts by faith; that ye, being rooted and grounded in love, May be able to comprehend with all saints what is the breadth, and length, and depth, and height; And to know the love of Christ, which passes knowledge, that ye might be filled with all the fullness of God."

Ephesians 3:14-19

"For this cause we also, since the day we heard it, do not cease to pray for you, and to desire that ye might be filled with the knowledge of his will in all wisdom and spiritual understanding; That ye might walk worthy of the Lord unto all pleasing, being fruitful in every good work, and increasing in the knowledge of God; Strengthened with all might, according to his glorious power, unto all patience and longsuffering with joyfulness."

- **Colossians 1:9-11**

These scriptures should be continuous prayer for you. When you pray these scriptures, you will be shocked at the depth of revelation knowledge you will begin to receive from God's Word as you read daily and also listen to messages of men of God.

Worry Not!

Let your prayers also seek to promote God's Kingdom. When you know His will and you have the opportunity to ask Him then you need not be worried. Worry and anxiety will only hinder you from hearing from God. You cannot have peace when you are worried.

For you to have peace even in hard and difficult situations, follow the instruction of Apostle Paul in his letter to the Philippian church.

> *"Don't worry about anything; instead, pray about everything; tell God your needs, and don't forget to thank him for his answers. 7 If you do this, you will experience God's peace, which is far more wonderful than the human mind can understand. His peace will keep your thoughts and your hearts quiet and at rest as you trust in Christ Jesus."*
>
> **-   Philippians 4:6-7**

He said not to worry about anything. Instead of worrying, talk to God concerning that situation, with the confidence that God will answer. Then thank Him for what He has done for you before. Many people don't know how to thank God. We should learn to appreciate God for everything He does for us.

Jesus Christ during His earthly ministry was a man of prayer and also taught about prayers. In Luke 5:16, the bible says Jesus often withdrew to the wilderness for prayers. He always took time to pray and the numerous miracles that accompanied his ministrations were proof of his prayer time with God.

Likewise, we ought to spend ample time in prayer. We should learn to settle issues on our knees. Every Christian should get to a stage in their Christian life, where they can hear God speak during their prayer time.

Communion with God is God's desire for His children.

> *"And this is my prayer: that your love may abound more and more and more in knowledge and depth of insight, so that you may be able to discern what is best and may be pure and blameless until the day of Christ, filled with the fruit of righteousness that comes through Jesus Christ- to the glory of and praise of God."*

> **Philippians 1:9-10**(NIV)

"May God himself, the God of peace, sanctify you through and through. May your whole spirit, soul and body be kept blameless at the coming of our Lord Jesus."

1 Thessalonians 5:23(NIV)

"Therefore we also pray always for you that our God would count you worthy of this calling, and fulfill all the good pleasure of His goodness and the work of faith with power, [12] that the name of our Lord Jesus Christ may be glorified in you, and you in Him, according to the grace of our God and the Lord Jesus Christ."

2 Thessalonians 1:11-12

"Now may our Lord Jesus Christ Himself, and our God and Father, who has loved us and given us everlasting consolation and good hope by grace, comfort your hearts and establish you in every good word and work."

2 Thessalonians 2:16-17

"Now may the God of peace who brought up our Lord Jesus from the dead, that great Shepherd of the sheep, through the blood of the everlasting covenant, make you complete in every good work to do His will, working in you what is well pleasing in His sight, through Jesus Christ, to whom be glory forever and ever. Amen."

- **Hebrews 13:20-21**

Praying in Tongues (1Cor.14:2, 4, 14 and 15)

During our prayers, we should endeavor to spend quality time praying in tongues. When we pray in tongues, we are talking to God, speaking by the power of the Spirit. When you pray in tongues, your spirit man is strengthened, making you fit for any spiritual battle. When you pray in tongues, your spirit is praying. You are speaking to God. This was the secret to Apostle Paul's success in ministry.

Jude 20(AMP)

But you, beloved, build yourselves up on [the foundation of] your most holy faith [continually progress, rise like an edifice higher and higher], pray in the Holy Spirit. Praying in the Holy Spirit helps us to build ourselves up.

The working power of the Holy Spirit in our lives as believers

1) Ephesians 3:20: (***Now to Him who is able to [carry out His purpose and] do superabundantly more than all that we dare ask or think [infinitely beyond our greatest prayers, hopes, or dreams], <u>according to His power that is at work within us</u>***) God is able to do exceedingly abundantly above all that we ask or think. How will God do this? Through the power of the Holy Spirit who dwells in us and who is working in us. The mighty power of God is at work in our lives. You activate that power when you pray in tongues. This is the language of the Spirit.

2) Romans 8:11. (***And if the Spirit of Him who raised Jesus from the dead lives in you, He who raised Christ Jesus from the dead will also <u>give life to your mortal bodies through His Spirit, who lives in you</u>***) If signifies that it is conditional. It depends on you to allow the Holy Spirit live in you. The question I want to ask you is, does the Spirit of God live in you? If your answer is yes, then that same Spirit has the power to give life to your mortal bodies. How can you activate this power for life and healing? It is through praying in tongues. This is the language of the Spirit.

3) Romans 8: 26-27 (***Likewise the Spirit also helps in our
weaknesses. For we do not know what we should pray for as
we ought, but the Spirit Himself makes intercession for us
with groanings which cannot be uttered.*** *²⁷* ***Now He who
searches the hearts knows what the mind of the Spirit is,
because He makes intercession for the saints according to the
will of God).***The Holy Spirit helps us to pray. How does it
happen? By praying in the language of the Spirit. Anytime you
are weak and you do not feel like praying, begin to pray in
tongues and the Holy Spirit will strengthen you and that
weakness will go. Again when you have an issue to pray about
and you do not know how to pray it in a known language, begin
to pray in tongues and the Holy Spirit will help you to present it
to God in the right manner. When you do this, your prayer life
will never remain the same again.

4)1 Corinthians 2:9-13(***But as it is written: "Eye has not seen, nor ear
heard, nor have entered into the heart of man the things which God has
prepared for those who love Him." But God has revealed them to us
through His Spirit. For the Spirit searches all things, yes, the deep things
of God. For what man knows the things of a man except the spirit of the
man which is in him? Even so no one knows the things of God except the
Spirit of God. Now we have received, not the spirit of the world, but the
Spirit who is from God, that we might know the things that have been
freely given to us by God. These things we also speak, not in words which
man's wisdom teaches but which the Holy Spirit teaches, comparing
spiritual things with spiritual***). You can get revelation into some deep things
concerning your life and family by praying in the language of the Spirit. When

you pray in the language of the Spirit, the Holy Spirit searches the mind of God and He will reveal whatever you desire to know. It is only the Spirit of God that knows the mind of God and if you want to know the mind of God concerning your life, marriage, career, business, family and many others, you get connected to the Holy Spirit to access the mind of God.

5)2 Corinthians 3:18. As we look into the mirror of God's word, we see or behold the glory of God (the image of God) and we are being transformed to the same image we are seeing. How can this transformation come? It is by the Spirit God (the Holy Spirit). When we look at the mirror of God's word, we do not see ourselves but the glory of God. As we continue to look at the image of God in that mirror of His word our image will begin to be transformed (changed) to that image we are seeing. As we begin to look, our image will be different from the image of God we are looking at, but as we continue our image will be changing to that image of God we are seeing. The image of God we see will not change to our own image but our image will change to God's image. The Holy Spirit is the catalyst of the change. Our duty is to continue to behold (look) at the image of God in the mirror of His word. It is not our duty to cause or make the transformation to take place, but it is the duty of the Holy Spirit. So don't think about how the transformation is going to take place, we just focus our mind and attention on looking.

Do we still need the Holy Spirit power today?

My answer is yes. In *Acts 2:38-39, says, then Peter said to them, "Repent, and let every one of you be baptized in the name of Jesus Christ for the remission of sins; and you shall receive the gift of the Holy Spirit. For the promise is to you and to your children, and to all who are afar off, as many as the Lord our God will call."* Peter said that the promise of the gift of the Holy Spirit for all who are afar off, as many as the Lord our God will call. We fall into this category of those that have been called by God.

 1 Peter 2:21 says that we should follow the example of Jesus. The example I want to look at here is how Jesus Christ related and cooperated with the Holy Spirit to accomplish His earthly mission.

First Jesus was Conceived & Born by the Holy Spirit. *Luke 1:35 "The Holy Spirit will come upon you, and the power of the Most High will overshadow you; therefore the child to be born will be called holy—the Son of God."* We need to be born of the Holy Spirit. That which is born of the flesh is flesh and that born of the Spirit is Spirit. The moment you give your life to Christ, you have been born of the Spirit. If you have not accepted Jesus Christ into your life, you can do that by inviting Him to come in to be your Lord and savior.

Again Jesus was baptized by the Holy Spirit for Life & Mission. *Luke 3:22 "...and the Holy Spirit descended on him in bodily form, like a dove; and a voice came from heaven, "You are my beloved Son; with you I am well pleased."* We need the baptism of the Holy Spirit for our lives and mission. This is baptism of the Holy Spirit with evidence of speaking in tongues. For you to live a successful and victorious Christian life, you need the baptism of the Holy Spirit.

Again Jesus was filled with & led by the Holy Spirit. Luke 4:1 *"And Jesus, full of the Holy Spirit, returned from the Jordan and was led by the Spirit in the wilderness"*

Again Jesus began His public teaching ministry empowered by the Holy Spirit. *Luke 4:14-15 "And Jesus returned in the power of the Spirit to Galilee, and a report about him went out through all the surrounding country. And he taught in the synagogues, being glorified by all."*

Again Jesus was empowered by the Holy Spirit to advance the gospel in word & deed. *Luke 4:18 "The Spirit of the Lord is upon me, because he has anointed me to proclaim good news to the poor. He has sent me to proclaim liberty to the captives and recovering of sight to the blind, to set at liberty those who are oppressed..."* We need the empowerment of the Holy Spirit to do the assignment God has given to us.

Again Jesus worshiped under the influence of the Holy Spirit. *Luke 10:21 In that same hour he rejoiced in the Holy Spirit and said, "I thank you, Father, Lord of heaven and earth, that you have hidden these things from the wise and understanding and revealed them to little children; yes, Father, for such was your gracious will.* We need to worship God under the influence of the Holy Spirit. We need to worship God in the Spirit because God is a Spirit and seek those that will worship Him in Spirit and in truth.

How can we receive the Baptism of the Holy Spirit?

In Luke 11:13, Jesus Christ said, If you then, being evil, know how to give good gifts to your children, how much more will *your* heavenly Father give the Holy Spirit to those who ask Him!". The answer is that you ask God for the Holy Spirit and He will gladly give Him to you. He made a promise in Joel 2:28, And it shall come to pass afterward That I will pour out My Spirit on all flesh; Your sons and your daughters shall prophesy, Your old men shall dream dreams, Your young men shall see visions. God made the promise and He is willing to fulfill His promise over your life. Remind Him of this promise in prayers.

Jesus Christ also reminded the Apostles of this promise in Luke 24:49, "Behold, I send the Promise of My Father upon you; but tarry in the city of Jerusalem until you are endued with power from on high." You need to tarry in prayer to receive the baptism of the Holy Spirit. When the Apostles tarried in Jerusalem, they received the promise of the Father. One major thing that was outstanding was the manifestation of speaking in another language (tongue). There is a school of thought that says, you can be baptized in the Holy Spirit and not speak in tongue. My candid advice is that we should strive to move higher in our walk with God and imitate the good things about the early Apostles. All of them spoke in tongues and many others they prayed for also experience the same.

Prayers Accompanied with Fasting

Fasting and prayer is a time you totally or partially abstain from food and water. Your aim is to dedicate yourself to time of prayer and fellowship with God. The Bible presents fasting as good, profitable, and beneficial. The book of Acts records believers fasting before they made important decisions (**Acts 13:2; 14:23**). Fasting and prayer are often linked together (**Luke 2:37; 5:33**). In the Old Testament, the Jews prominent reason for fasting was to display sincere mourning in order to avert God's wrath. The goal is to humble oneself before God and to seek his face in prayer. Having a dedicated time of prayer and fasting is not a way of manipulating God into doing what you desire.

Rather, it is simply forcing yourself to focus and rely on God for the strength, provision, and wisdom you need. Will your fasting and prayer make God to answer you faster? NO, but it will help you to position yourself spiritually to hear and receive from God.

Occasions for fasting in the Bible

1) To prepare to receive God's law : Ex. 34:28
2) To show sorrow at the time of death: 1 Sam. 31:13
3) To show sorrow for sin: 1 Kings 21:17
4) To show humility : Psalm 35:13
5) To pray in time of national need : 2 chronicles 20:3, Esther 4:16
6) To accomplish deep personal prayer 2 Sam. 12:16
7) A regular pattern for many Jews: Matthew 9:14
8) Paul after his conversion : Acts 9:9
9) To prepare for mission work: Acts 13:2-3
10) To prepare for ministry : Matthew 4:2

There are two major types of fast: The total and partial fasting. The total fast is when you totally abstain from food and water for the period of the fast. The partial fast is when you do not eat food but take water or fruit for the period of the fast. The number of days you decide to take a fast is dependent on you and possibly by God's divine instruction. For health reasons, total or dry fast should not be longer than eight days (except divinely instructed).

The Daniel Fast: Origin

The Daniel fast is based on verses from the Bible found in **Daniel 10:2-3**. "*At that time I, Daniel, mourned for three weeks. I ate no choice food; no meat or wine touched my lips; and I used no lotions at all until the three weeks were over.*" These three weeks refer to the observance of Passover and the Feast of Unleavened Bread, which take place during the first month of the year **(Exodus 12:1-20)**.

Some people may also cite the example in Daniel 1:8. However, in this verse, Daniel did not eat the king's delicacies because it would have included food that was forbidden by the Mosaic Law (**Leviticus 11**); and to eat it would be defiling his body. Another reason would have been because the king's meats had probably been dedicated to the false Babylonian idols as was their practice. Daniel believed to do so would have been to acknowledge their idols as deities, against God's commandments.

The Daniel Fast: Purpose

While the Daniel fast cleanses the body by omitting certain foods for a limited time, the deeper and true basis of intent is for spiritual connection. The purpose of Christian fasting is to seek a more intimate relationship with God while ridding your physical body of unnatural, self-gratifying food and drink. Your focus is to be on God, not on the fleshly things of the world. Too often, the focus of fasting is on the lack of food. Instead, the **fasting should** be to take your eyes off the things of this world, to focus completely on God.

During the Daniel fast, you will want to concentrate on prayer, bible study, and reflection. The Daniel fast is a great way to enter into preparation for growing in the Lord.

If you have a medical condition or are undergoing any medical treatments, it is advisable to first consult your physician. You may also want to pray, consult a mature Christian or your pastor before fasting. Remember, fasting should be periodic and for limited days.

The Daniel Fast: Guideline

The basic guideline for the Daniel fast includes eating:

- Fruits and nuts

- Vegetables

- Water only (to flush out toxins) Some say natural fruit juices may be included if they contain no preservatives, sugar, etc., but even those juices should be very limited. Coffee and tea are not permitted.

The Daniel fast should eliminate all meats, pastries, chips, breads, and fried foods. Breads contain yeast, baking powder and so on; those are leavening agents and should be avoided. Leaven is symbolic of sin in certain scriptures (**1 Corinthians 5:6-8**).

With these things listed, it is concluded that any food having artificial additives, chemicals, or that is processed should be totally avoided during the fast. Fruits and vegetables are the mainstay of the Daniel fast and can be acceptably prepared in a variety of ways. There are many fasting recipes and several cookbooks designed for the Daniel fast.

The Daniel fast is a powerful spiritual discipline. With the coupling of fasting and prayer, one can open himself to God's Holy Spirit. Having a sincere desire to seek God, you can come to Him with a contrite and repentant heart and He will minister to you in a powerful way. God's awesome power is transforming and you will know that with God, all things are possible.

It is important to note that the Bible in no way commands believers to observe a Daniel fast. As a result, it is a matter of Christian freedom whether to observe it or not. (Source: Mark and Patti Virkler, " Fulfill your financial Destiny", How to Hear God's voice" (Published by Communication with God Ministries, 1999, 2001)

Encouraging Bible Verses on Prayer

2 Chronicles 7:14

"If my people, who are called by my name, will humble themselves and pray and seek my face and turn from their wicked ways, then will I hear from heaven and will forgive their sin and will heal their land."

Psalm 4:1

"Answer me when I call to you, O my righteous God. Give me relief from my distress; be merciful to me and hear my prayer."

Psalm 5:3

"My voice You shall hear in the morning, O LORD; in the morning I will direct my prayer to You, and I will look up."

Psalm 50:15

"Call upon me in the day of trouble; I will deliver you, and you will honor me."

Psalm 55:17

"Evening and morning, and at noon, I will pray and cry aloud; and He shall hear my voice."

Psalm 65:1-2

"Praise awaits you, our God, in Zion; to you our vows will be fulfilled. You who answer prayer, to you all people will come."

Psalms 145:18

"The LORD is near to all who call on him, to all who call on him in truth."

Matthew 6:5-12

"And when you pray, do not be like the hypocrites, for they love to pray standing in the synagogues and on the street corners to be seen by men. I tell you the truth, they have received their reward in full. But when you pray, go into your room, close the door and pray to your Father, who is unseen. Then your Father, who sees what is done in secret, will reward you. And when you pray, do not keep on babbling like pagans, for they think they will be heard because of their many words. Do not be like them, for your Father knows what you need before you ask him. "This, then, is how you should pray: "'Our Father in heaven, hallowed be your name, your kingdom come, your will be done on earth as it is in heaven. Give us today our daily bread. Forgive us our debts, as we also have forgiven our debtors."

Matthew 7:7-8

"Ask and it will be given to you; seek and you will find; knock and the door will be opened to you. For everyone who asks

receives; he who seeks finds; and to him who knocks, the door will be opened."

Matthew 7:11

"If you, then, though you are evil, know how to give good gifts to your children, how much more will your Father in heaven give good gifts to those who ask Him!"

Mark 9:28-29

"After Jesus had gone indoors, his disciples asked him privately, "Why couldn't we drive it out?" He replied, "This kind can come out only by prayer."

1Timothy 2:8

"I want men everywhere to lift up holy hands in prayer, without anger or disputing."

Hebrews 4:16

"Let us then approach the throne of grace with confidence, so that we may receive mercy and find grace to help us in our time of need."

James 1:7

"But when he asks, he must believe and not doubt, because he who doubts is like a wave of the sea, blown and tossed by the wind. That man should not think he will receive anything from the Lord;"

Some questions to ponder on:

How are you committed to God in prayer? Do you pray long enough to breakthrough? Have you birthed your vision and dream through prayers? Have you been a watchman over your family, business, career, marriage, ministry, job through prayers? Have you persisted in prayers to that point that heaven has no other choice than to respond to you.

CHAPTER FOUR

FELLOWSHIP

What is fellowship?

According to Longman's Dictionary of Contemporary English, fellowship is a group of people who share an interest or belief, especially Christians who have religious ceremonies together.

Who can we have fellowship with?

"That which we have seen and heard declare we unto you, that ye also may have fellowship with us: and truly our fellowship is with the Father, and with his Son Jesus Christ.

Verse 7-But if we walk in the light, as he is in the light, we have fellowship one with another, and the blood of Jesus Christ his Son cleanses us from all sin."

\-   *1 John 1:3,7*

Our fellowship is with both God and Man. Our fellowship with God enables us have fellowship with our brothers and sisters in Christ. Without good fellowship with our brethren, we cannot have good fellowship with God. Apostle John says in 1 John 2:9-10, that we cannot claim to be children of the light and hate our brother, because when we do, we are in darkness. Again in chapter 4:7, Apostle John encourages us to love one another because God is love and when we love this way, it shows that we are born of God.

As Erwin Lutzer wrote in his book, **How to say no to stubborn habits**, "We cannot successfully live the Christian life on our own. God never intended that any one of us experience either failure or success alone, independent of the body of Christ. We need God's people for encouragement and intercession and for the strength that come from close fellowship."

The bible records that the believers in the early church lived like one large family.

> *"And all that believed were together, and had all things common; And sold their possessions and goods, and parted them to all men, as every man had need. And they, continuing daily with one accord in the temple, and breaking bread from house to house, did eat their meat with gladness and singleness of heart."*

"And the multitude of them that believed were of one heart and of one soul: neither said any of them that ought of the things which he possessed was his own; but they had all things common. And with great power gave the apostles witness of the resurrection of the Lord Jesus: and great grace was upon them all. Neither was there any among them that lacked: for as many as were possessors of lands or houses sold them, and brought the prices of the things that were sold, And laid them down at the apostles' feet: and distribution was made unto every man according as he had need. And Joses, who by the apostles was surnamed Barnabas, (which is, being interpreted, The son of consolation,) a Levite, and of the country of Cyprus, Having land, sold it, and brought the money, and laid it at the apostles' feet."

Today, the Church needs believers whose hearts are after God and are willing, sacrificial givers to those suffering in our churches. We need to emulate and imitate the early Church in their concern for the needy. When we care for their needs, it will bring fear on the world around us because unbelievable signs and wonders will accompany.

We should also fellowship with our family, which include father, mother, brothers and sisters, husband with wife, children and parents.

Our greatest expression of fellowship and the highest principle for relationships should be love. Since God first loved us, we ought to demonstrate love toward one another. (1 John 3:11, 16, 18; 4:7-21) For the purpose of this book I have identified the following specific expressions of love as being among the most desirable.

- **Building Up One Another**: We expect each member of the church or family to strive consciously to maintain relationships that support, encourage and build up one another. (Romans 15:1-2)

- **Making Allowance for One Another**: Because of our fallenness, difficulties in relationships do occur. In such cases we are to respond with compassion, kindness, humility, gentleness and patience, making allowance for each other and forgiving one another. (Colossians 3:12-13)

- **Caring for One Another**: We are responsible to come alongside those experiencing grief, discouragement, illness, tragedy, or other personal trials. Expressions of bearing one another's burdens include comfort, encouragement, consolation and intercession. (Galatians 6:2)

- **Respecting One Another**: Because of the God-given worth and dignity of persons, each member of the church or family is expected to be sensitive to the image of God created in every person. Therefore, discrimination against others on the basis of race, national origin, age, gender or disability should not be accepted. Any kind of demeaning gesture, symbol, communication, threat or act of violence directed toward another person should be named among us. (Colossians 3:11-14; 1 John 3:14-18)

- **Speaking the Truth in Love**: A church or family can be strengthened by speaking the truth to each other with love. Problems in relationships and behavior can be resolved constructively by confronting one another in an appropriate spirit. If the welfare of the one being confronted is paramount and if the confronter is motivated by and acting in love, the process can produce growth. (Ephesians 4:15)

Where to Fellowship?

The Bible talks about the Church that met at homes (house fellowship). At the same time, it makes mention of the gathering together of God's people in the temple(church fellowship).

What is the Church?

The Church means a 'called out' people. Being part of the 'called out 'people guarantee you a testimony.

To be committed in church means that you are not just a Sunday-Sunday attendee; midweek services matter too. Not only that, it is not enough to attend; you have to be involved in the activities within the local assembly. The bible says in **Hebrew 10:25,** "N*ot forsaking the assembling of ourselves together, as the manner of some is; but exhorting one another: and so much the more, as ye see the day approaching.*"

The writer of Hebrews encourages us not to neglect the gathering of the saints as some people do. When things are not going fine with them, some people tend to neglect the fellowship of brethren. It is not supposed to be so. Attend church, whether things are okay or not. To be committed to God, it is necessary to find your roots and be planted in the house of God.

There are many reasons we need to fellowship with one another.

Number one, the bible says iron sharpens iron. When you are in fellowship with other saints, there are words of encouragement from their testimonies that can boost your faith.

Secondly, you can learn from other believers and get godly advice from them as well. The Lord can speak to you through prophecy as it happened in **Acts 21:10-12:**

> *"And as we tarried there many days, there came down from Judaea a certain prophet, named Agabus. And when he was come unto us, he took Paul's girdle, and bound his own hands and feet, and said, Thus saith the Holy Ghost,*

> *So shall the Jews at Jerusalem bind the man that owned this girdle, and shall deliver him into the hands of the Gentiles. And when we heard these things, both we, and they of that place, besought him not to go up to Jerusalem."*

Evil plans of the enemy can be revealed through the gift of revelation operating in the lives of other believers around you. The reason for the spiritual gifts given to the church is not to show superiority but so that everyone can benefit from them.

> *"And he gave some, apostles; and some, prophets; and some, evangelists; and some, pastors and teachers; For the perfecting of the saints, for the work of the ministry, for the edifying of the body of Christ: Till we all come in the unity of the faith, and of the knowledge of the Son of God, unto a perfect man, unto the measure of the stature of the fullness of Christ:*

That we henceforth be no more children, tossed to and fro, and carried about with every wind of doctrine, by the sleight of men, and cunning craftiness, whereby they lie in wait to deceive; But speaking the truth in love, may grow up into him in all things, which is the head, even Christ: From whom the whole body fitly joined together and compacted by that which every joint supplieth, according to the effectual working in the measure of every part maketh increase of the body unto the edifying of itself in love."

- Eph.4:11–16

From this scripture, we can see that:

1. The gifts equip believers to do God's work
2. Through fellowship you can be mature and fully grow in the Lord.
3. When you are mature, you will not be like a child who normally changes his mind in every situation anymore.
4. It is through fellowship that you can discover your God given assignment on this earth.

Beloved, if you are out of fellowship, you cannot enjoy these benefits.

In the gathering of God's people, we can partake in the Holy Communion.

"The righteous shall flourish like a palm tree; he shall grow like a cedar in Lebanon. Those who are <u>planted</u> in the house of the Lord shall flourish in the courts of our God. They shall still be bearing fruit in old age; they shall be fresh and flourishing."

-   **Ps. 92: 12 – 14**

The psalmist in verse 13 here talks about being planted in the house of God. The word 'planted' or 'transplanted' as used by the *New Living* translation, means to put in the ground in order for it to grow. The ground here represents the church. The purpose of planting any seed in the soil is for growth and there are conditions for growth. Basically speaking, the church is where you can get the necessary conditions for spiritual growth. Without the church, a believer cannot grow in the Christian race. When you are planted in the house of God, you will flourish even in your old age. You will continue to bear fruits till God calls you home.

Church Activities

"And they continued steadfastly in the apostles' doctrine and fellowship, and in breaking of bread, and in prayers."

-   **Acts 2: 42**

There are four (4) major Church activities that you need to be part of. There are others which your church may add and this varies from church to church, but these four are key:

1. Bible Study

Different churches give it different names. This is the time to do a deep search into the scriptures for proper understanding of the word of God. Here, you are told how to apply these teachings to your life situations. This is what the bible calls the Apostles' teachings. The bible says the early believers devoted themselves to the apostles' teachings. You too have to devote your time to these scriptures to see the importance of the word of God. Proverbs 4:20 – 22, 8:17 – 21; 2 Tim.2:15, Acts 20:32, Joshua 1:8; Col. 3:16

2. Prayer Meeting

Prayer meeting is the second activity you should be part of. Many people do not like prayers. As earlier mentioned, many prayers are not answered because they are not said according to the will of God.

The early apostles always attended prayer meetings (Acts 3:1, 4:23–31).

The Church body prayed prayers of agreement (Acts 12:12, 13:1–3).

During prayer meetings, we intercede for men, kings, government, missionaries, and many others.

3. Holy Communion Service (Breaking of Bread)

According to Acts 2:42, the bible says the early believers gathered for the breaking of bread. This is very important because, Jesus Christ gave us an instruction to frequently do this in remembrance of His death and resurrection.

"For I have received of the Lord that which also I delivered unto you, That the Lord Jesus the same night in which he was betrayed took bread: And when he had given thanks, he brake it, and said, Take, eat: this is my body, which is broken for you: this do in remembrance of me. After the same manner also he took the cup, when he had supped, saying, This cup is the new testament in my blood: this do ye, as oft as ye drink it, in remembrance of me. For as often as ye eat this bread, and drink this cup, ye do shew the Lord's death till he come."

- 1 Corinthians 11:17–34

Holy Communion Service is a time to eat the body (bread) and drink the blood (wine) of Jesus. The bread is not the body of Christ per se, but we use it to represent His body. The wine represents His blood. Jesus said in John 6:47–58 that the bread is his flesh which we must eat to live and the wine, his blood which we must drink to have life. The life of an animal is in its blood therefore the life of Jesus is in His blood. If you want to have the life of Jesus, you have to take part in the communion service.

What qualifies you to receive communion is being born again. Once you have received Jesus Christ as your Lord and personal Savior, then you qualify. Also, do self-examination, if there is any way you have sinned or offended God and man, you should immediately ask God for forgiveness before taking the communion.

Jesus is our advocate before the Father (1 John1:1-2). He comes before the Father and asks for mercy on our behalf.

4.   Fellowship (Sunday Morning Worship)

We must give our time for Sunday worship service. This is a fellowship, where we enter into the presence of God in reverence. During this service, God can do anything in righteousness, so it is not a time to play games. Here, a word of instruction can come forth, and gifts of the spirit such as word of wisdom, word of knowledge, miracles, prophecy, etc. can manifest.

In the course of the worship service, solutions to people's problems are unveiled – releasing a word that will give direction, leading, guidance, wisdom and miracles. During our services, we should allow the Holy Spirit to do His work in our lives. From the beginning, the intention of God was to have fellowship with man - have a good time with man.

Benefits of Belonging to a Local Assembly/Church

1.   It identifies you as a genuine believer – Ephesians. 2:19, Romans. 12:5

As you join a local assembly, you will no longer be a stranger to the body of Christ. You automatically become a member of the household of God, through your membership in a local church. You will begin to enjoy the covenant blessings that other saints enjoy. You cannot enjoy these benefits when you refuse to identify with a local church.

2.   As you fellowship with other Christians, you have access to some blessings that you could not have gotten on your own. Sometime ago, a situation occurred whereby I urgently needed the services of a lawyer. For me to get one, I needed some money, which I did not have at that critical time. But a member of my local assembly, a lawyer by profession, helped me out without collecting a dime. The services he rendered would have cost me some good money.

3.   The local church provides a spiritual family to support and encourage you in your walk with Christ (Gal. 6:1-2). In the local assembly or church, there is always spiritual help peradventure one is over taken by any sin or fault. What could have made you suffer spiritual affliction would be handled with love and help you navigate your way out.

4.   The Bible also encourages us to bear one another's burden for this is to fulfill the law of Christ. Heb. 10: 24 – 25. We can easily perform this function in the local church, caring about the welfare of the flock of God.

5.   In the local church, we can stir one another up in love and towards good works. Brethren can inspire one another to continue in love and do good works towards God and man.

6.   The local church provides you a place to discover and use your gift in ministry.

        1   Corinthians 12:4-27

7.   The local church gives you the opportunity to be under the spiritual protection of godly leaders. Heb. 13:17, Acts 20: 28-29.

The leaders in the church are there to help you. They are shepherds and are mandated to give you direction in life. They are sent by God to take care of your spiritual needs and as a matter of fact, will give account of each soul He sends to them.

Your duty is to obey and be submissive to them. Please allow them to do the work God has given them with joy, and not grief.
I want to say this here, that if you are under the ministry of a man you do not believe in, there is no way you can be blessed. You have to believe in your pastor. If you have any grudge or resentment, try and find a way to resolve it as soon as possible. You cannot be bitter against the authority set over you.

Who Is Your Spiritual Father/Mother? It's very important!
I believe that each believer needs a spiritual father and/or mother. First comes the natural and then the spiritual. As we all have biological parents so we should give ourselves to spiritual parents as well. It could be either a spiritual father or mother, or both. More than that leads to division and double mindedness.
A spiritual father covers and nurtures the son. He carries the son forever in his heart and prayers. A spiritual father never abandons son. A spiritual father makes room in his life for inviting the son to accompany and join him on special events and activities. He makes the son feel like he is legitimately part of the family with full privileges.

Likewise, a son honors his spiritual father. A son comes home often. He takes responsibility for calling and contacting his spiritual father often with news of how he is doing. He delights in keeping his spiritual father up to date concerning his life.

Also, a son carries the vision of the spiritual father and sees to it that the vision never dies and that it is fully completed. He is a defender of the faith of his spiritual father.

A true son gladly and generously supports his spiritual father so that the father can minister to other sons in the family, some of whom might be in trouble one way or the other.

Parent-Child Connection

God has opened the hearts of sons and daughters, who have needed a "home". You see, a son or daughter must first appear or be manifested before there can be a father and mother. These sons and daughters whom God has given open hearts are now ready to receive fathers and mothers. They are ready to "get connected" to their "home."

"Therefore you are no longer a slave, but a son; and if a son, then an heir through God." - **Galatians 4:7**

God has raised up anointed apostolic fathers and mothers, who will offer a "home base" for those who have had enough of life and ministry without it.

"And I will be a father to you, and you shall be sons and daughters to Me," says *the Lord Almighty."*- **2 Corinthians 6:18**

"For if you were to have countless tutors in Christ, yet you would not have many fathers; for in Christ Jesus I became your father through the gospel. I exhort you

therefore, be imitators of me. For this reason I have sent to you Timothy, who is my beloved and faithful child in the Lord, and he will remind you of my ways which are in Christ, just as I teach everywhere in every church." - **1 Corinthians 4:15-17**

Humble Apostolic Fathers and Mothers

God does not want spiritual dictators or authoritarians. He wants meek, humble apostolic fathers and mothers for the young and upcoming children of God.

When God gets a spiritual father and mother connecting in a "home base" relationship with sons and daughters, the day is over for the lone eagle in the desert and dry creek beds. A new day is dawning.

Humble Oversight Occurs in Meaningful and Blessed Relationships

In a "home base" atmosphere, deep friendships occur that last for a lifetime. Family is forever. Yes, we have disagreements and differing opinions about things. But we never forget the most important thing. Families love each other and never, under God, leave each other.

Jesus as our role model, had children whom He nurtured in His three and half years of ministry. We popularly call them the twelve disciples. How did He get these spiritual sons? The bible tells us that He selected, called them to Himself the particular people he wanted.

> *"And He went up to the mountain and summoned those whom He Himself wanted, and they came to Him"* **-Mark 3:13**

Hence, He evangelized them and He thereafter became their pastor.

The Pastor - A Spiritual Father

Your pastor is your spiritual father therefore you need to seek his blessings in whatever you want to do. No matter the cost, do not commonize the father's blessing. Seek your pastor's blessing as a spiritual father because it is very important. In **Gen. 27:34, 38,**Esau begged his father to bless him. It was through the pronouncement of the father that he discovered how he could come out of bondage.

In verse 40, his father gave him the secret to his deliverance:*"And it shall come to pass, when you become restless, that you shall break his yoke from your neck."* (NKJV)

This was how Esau came out of poverty and became wealthy. He was so blessed that he told Jacob that he had more than enough. My prayer for you is that you will get to that position where you will confess and declare that you have more than enough.

NOTE:

A Christian without a home church is like an organ without a body, a branch without a tree, a sheep without a flock or a child without a family.

If you are not yet a committed member of any church, I will like to encourage you to do so. Don't be a spiritual bastard. You must have a spiritual father. Look for a church that you can identify with. Look for a church, where the word of God is taught and practiced; where the word of God is the final say.

A purpose-driven church is what you need, which meets your spiritual and physical needs. I pray that the Lord will open your eyes to see one.

Let me warn here that you should not be looking for a perfect church with perfect people because no such church exists. Every church is filled with imperfect people working with a perfect God.

CHAPTER FIVE

TELL OTHERS ABOUT JESUS

"And Jesus came and spoke to them, saying, "All authority has been given to Me in heaven and on earth. Go therefore and make disciples of all the nations, baptizing them in the name of the Father and of the Son and of the Holy Spirit, teaching them to observe all things that I have commanded you; and lo, I am with you always, even to the end of the age." Amen.

-   Matt.28:18-20

Every believer in Christ has been given the mandate to preach the gospel, to tell others about Jesus Christ. This is not optional. It is a command from Jesus to all of us - to preach what He, Christ, came to accomplish for us. In our preaching, it is good that we are able to give sound reasons why everyone needs Jesus Christ in their life. This ability will help us bring many souls to Christ.

Take the example of Philip, who used the scripture that the Ethiopian Eunuch was reading to preach the goodness about Christ. He used this and other scriptures to proclaim Christ. (Acts 8:35)

Before leaving His disciples, Jesus told them that He would send the Comforter, who would tell them more about Him (Jesus).And then they (the disciples) could also tell others about Him.
It is the same Comforter who will give the power to be able to tell others (evangelize).

> *"And ye shall receive power after that the Holy Ghost is come upon you and ye shall be my witnesses...."*
> **- Acts 1:8**

We need the power of the Holy Spirit in order to witness to people. It is the Holy Spirit that convinces the hearer to accept the message of salvation that is preached. Without the Spirit of God, no individual can win souls for Christ. It is how God draws men to Jesus.

The Holy Spirit also gives boldness to proclaim the gospel. Look at Peter, who denied our Lord Jesus three times before His crucifixion. On the day of Pentecost, after he had received the Holy Spirit baptism, he became bold in declaring the death and resurrection of Jesus (Acts 2:37.)The bible records that the words of Peter convicted the people so deeply that they asked what they must do to be saved. It was not Peter, but the power of the Holy Spirit at work in him. This is one of the reasons the Holy Spirit was sent to us (Jn. 16:5-15).

The job of teaching others about Christ is for all believers. We should not fail to proclaim the goodness of God in our work places. You may not have time to be going from one place to the other but you can at least tell others about Christ at work or your business place. Preach to the people that you meet on a daily basis.

When preaching, we can warn people as occasion arises, but not condemn them. If wisdom is not applied, we may end up driving the people far away into the world, instead of drawing them close to Christ.

In 2 Tim.1:8, Paul advised Timothy not to be ashamed of proclaiming the gospel. In the same vein, you also might encounter some suffering for the gospel's sake, but don't let this stop you from telling others about Christ. Apostle Paul was not ashamed of preaching the gospel. He called the preaching of the gospel an obligation to him (Rom. 1:16).

Brothers and sisters in Christ, if you want to always have testimony, you should learn to tell others about Christ.

If you have not been discipled, trained and empowered, please submit yourself to your pastor for training, in order to be equipped for the work. It is an important and interesting assignment which we must be part of. It is the Great Commission. Commit yourself to it and you will see God at work in your life and your local assembly.

The bible says that he who wins a soul is wise. Be a wise brother, be a wise sister! Heaven rejoices over one sinner that is converted. Let heaven rejoice whenever you bring in lost souls. God bless you as you do so in Jesus' Name. Amen.

You must be determined to work hard to see that souls are won into the Kingdom of God. Evangelism requires hard work and self-discipline. Our effort shows us as part of those seeking and saving the lost souls. This is the primary purpose why Jesus came to the world. He came to seek and to save those who are lost (Luke 19:10).

What is The Message?

As you evangelize, do not preach any other message except Jesus Christ. Your message should be centered on Christ.

In 2 Cor. 4:5, Paul said, they preached Christ Jesus and not themselves. Many people today do not preach Christ but themselves. They talk about their connections and how rich their families are. Some preach to condemn others, others preach to justify themselves. All these are wrong. If you don't preach Christ, how can the people believe in Him so that they can call on Him? How can they call on Him to save them except they hear and how can they hear of him except someone (you) tell them about him?

Your part in the salvation of unbelievers is to simply preach Christ so that they can believe and call on Him for their salvation. Whatever title you give to your message, the center point should still be Christ Jesus.

You are to preach the power of God unto salvation. Paul said in Romans 1: 16-17 that the Good News about Christ is the power of God at work, saving everyone who believes. Tell them how they can be made right with God through the Good News of Christ. Let them know that their salvation is accomplished totally by faith, from start to finish.

Don't give them a false gospel of coming to Jesus so they can be rich. They should come to Jesus because they need salvation and deliverance. As they seek the Kingdom of God first, every other thing will be added (Matt.6:33). But if they come because of the other things, they may be disappointed. There are people who have stopped attending church today because when they were preached to, they were told that as soon as they accept Jesus, their sufferings will be over. This set of people did not accept Jesus because of salvation, but because they want their sufferings to be over. After spending some years in the church and their sufferings remain unchanged, disappointment sets in.

Tell them there is salvation in the gospel, there is healing in the gospel, there is prosperity in the gospel, there is deliverance in the gospel etc. Tell them the mandate of Jesus Christ to preach good news to the poor, the captives, the blind, and the broken hearted

> *"So He came to Nazareth, where He had been brought up. And as His custom was, He went into the synagogue on the Sabbath day, and stood up to read. And He was handed the book of the prophet Isaiah. And when He had opened the book, He found the place where it was written: "The Spirit of the LORD is upon Me, Because He has anointed Me To preach the gospel to the poor; He has sent Me to heal the brokenhearted, To proclaim liberty to the captives And recovery of sight to the blind, To set at liberty those who are oppressed; To proclaim the acceptable year of the LORD."*- **Luke 4:16–19**

We Must Use God's Word

To win souls, we must know how to use the Word of God. Just as a doctor does not give the same prescription to every patient, so the same verse will not meet the need of every person. You must have a good working knowledge of the Bible.

Are you reading your Bible daily? Are you memorizing scriptures? Have you established your quiet time? Do not neglect these things if you want to win souls.

Four Basic Truths

There are four basic truths in the gospel message:

1) The fact of sin.

2) The penalty of sin.

3) Christ paid the penalty.

4) We must receive Christ.

 Get these four facts firmly fixed in your mind, because you will use them in leading souls to Christ.

How to Lead a Person to Christ

1) Show him that he is a sinner. Key Verse: Romans 3:23

In leading someone to Christ, you simply explain the four basic truths of the gospel.

The first step in leading a person to Christ is to show him from God's Word that he is a sinner. A good passage to use for this is Romans 3:10—12. Let him read these verses.

*As it is written: **"There is none righteous, no, not one;[11] There is none who understands; There is none who seeks after God.[12] They have all turned aside;***
They have together become unprofitable; There is none who does good, no, not one."

This is what God says about us. Now have him read Romans 3:23. Before a person can be saved, he must realize that he is a sinner and be willing to give up his sins. The Lord Jesus said,

"Unless you repent, you will all likewise perish." Luke 13:5

2) **Show him that the penalty of sin is death. Key Verse: Romans 6:23**

The next step is to show him from God's Word that the penalty of sin is death. "For the wages of sin is death...." Explain that the word "death" as used here means separation from God, in the lake of fire, forever. Because we are sinners and condemned to eternal death, we need a Saviour.

3) **Show him that Christ died to pay the penalty of our sins. Key verse: John 3:16**

Our next verse is a very familiar one—John 3:16. Let him read it. Who does God mean when He says "the world"? He means every one. This includes you and me.

What did God give to us? He gave His Son to us. This means that He gave Jesus to die on the cross for our sins.

Why did God give us a Saviour? Because He loves us and because we need a Saviour! We cannot save ourselves, so God gave Jesus to us to be our Saviour.

If I give you something, do you have to pay me for it? No. Do you have to work for it? No. But there is one thing you must do—you must receive it. God has given the Lord Jesus to us to be our Saviour, but we must receive Him.

4) **Ask him to receive Christ as his Savior. Key verse: John 1:12**

Now turn to John 1:12. Have him read this verse. How does one become a child of God? By receiving the Lord Jesus. "As many as received Him, to them He gave the right to become children of God...."

Now you can ask these questions: Do you believe that Jesus Christ is the Son of God? Do you believe that He died on the cross for your sins and rose again? Do you believe that He is able to save you? Do you believe that He is willing to save you? Do you believe that He would come into your heart and save you right now if you asked Him to?

If the answer to these questions is "Yes," then you can ask, "Would you like to ask the Lord Jesus to come into your heart right now? If so, then pray this prayer with me:

"Lord Jesus, I know that I am a sinner. I believe that You are the Son of God, and that You died on the cross for my sins. Please come into my heart right now, and be my Saviour."

Knowing That You Are Saved

When a person truly receives Christ as his Saviour, God wants him to know that he is saved. How can a person know that he is saved? He can know (1) by believing God's Word, and (2) by the witness of the Holy Spirit.

A good verse to use for assurance is John 3:36. Note that God speaks of two groups of people in this verse—those who believe on the Son, and those who do not believe on Him.

God said it!

I believe it!

That settles it!

What does God say about those who believe on the Son? He says, "He who believes on the Son has everlasting life." The word "has" means that you have it—right now! Now read 1 John 5:11, 12 and 13. Notice in these verses that God says we CAN KNOW that we have eternal life.

Assurance of salvation also comes from the witness of the Holy Spirit. This simply means that the Holy Spirit lets us know in our spirit that we are saved. The Bible says,

"The Spirit Himself bears witness with our spirit, that we are children of God."

- Romans 8:16

How can we know that another person is saved? We cannot know for sure. We may sincerely believe that a person has received Christ as his Saviour, but we may be mistaken. For this reason, we should never tell a person that he is saved. This is the work of the Holy Spirit.

How to deal with objections

Use your Bible to deal with objections

1) "I am not a great sinner."

Answer: God says that we are all sinners.

"For all have sinned, and come short of the glory of God." **Romans 3:23**

2) "I'm a Baptist...a Methodist...a Catholic, etc."

Answer: Church membership does not save anyone—you must be born again. Jesus said,

"Unless a man is born again, he cannot see the kingdom of God." **John 3:3**

3) "There are hypocrites in the church."

Answer: Yes, there are, but there will be no hypocrites in Heaven. You will not be judged by what someone else did, but by your own life. The Bible says,

"So then every one of us shall give account of himself to God." **Romans 14:12**

4) "I would have to give up too much."

Answer: If you are not willing to give up your sins, you will be lost forever. Is it worth this? Jesus said,

*"For what shall it profit a man, if he shall gain the whole world, and lose his own soul?"***Mark 8:36**

5) "I am waiting until I become better."

Answer: You can't make yourself better. The Lord Jesus tells us to come to Him just as we are, and He promises to receive us. He said,

"...the one who comes to Me I will by no means cast out." **John 6:37**

6) "I am afraid I can't live the Christian life."

Answer: No one can—until Christ comes to live in him. He enables us to live the Christian life. The Apostle Paul said,

*"I can do all things through Christ who strengthens me."***Philippians 4:13**

7) "I am too great a sinner."

Answer: Jesus came to save sinners. He will save anyone who comes to Him. The Apostle Paul said,

*"This is a faithful saying and worthy of all acceptance, that Christ Jesus came into the world to save sinners, of whom I am chief."***I Timothy 1:15**

8) "I am doing the best I can."

Answer: We are not saved by our good works, but through faith in Christ.

*"For by grace you have been saved through faith, and that not of yourselves; it is the gift of God, not of works, lest anyone should boast."***Ephesians 2:8,9**

9) "I think one way is as good as another so long as you are sincere."

Answer: You may be sincere, but you may be sincerely wrong. The Bible says,

*"There is a way that seems right to a man, but its end is the way of death."***Proverbs 14:12**

Jesus is the Saviour—the only Saviour. We cannot come to God except by Him. Jesus said,

*"I am the way, the truth, and the life: no one comes to the Father, but by Me."***John 14:6**

10)"Maybe later."

Answer: It is dangerous to put off so important a matter. The Bible says,

*"Do not boast about tomorrow, for you do not know what a day may bring forth."***Proverbs 27:1**

11)"I don't want to give up my sins."

Answer: Then you will be lost forever. Jesus said,

"Unless you repent, you will all likewise perish." **Luke 13:5**

12)"I don't believe in hell."

Answer: This does not change the fact of hell. The Bible says,

> *"But the cowardly, unbelieving, abominable, murderers, sexually immoral, sorcerers, idolaters, and all liars, shall have their part in the lake which burns with fire and brimstone..."*- **Revelation 21:8**

(Memorize these objections and the answers so you will know them when you need them.)

Some Do's and Don'ts

DO
always use your Bible when leading people to Christ. Even though you may be able to quote the verse, it is better to let the other person read it himself.

DON'T
use too many verses.

DO
look to God in prayer for the guidance of the Holy Spirit.

DON'T
interrupt people. Try to find out their problem, but don't get side-tracked. Keep bringing them back to the matter of their relationship to the Lord Jesus.

DO

be earnest. This is no time for joking. Soul-winning is serious business.

DON'T

argue. God does not send us out to win arguments; He sends us out to win souls.

DO

be careful of your breath. Don't offend people needlessly.

DO

admit it when you don't know the answer to a question. Just say, "I don't know the answer to that question, but I am sure there must be one. One thing I do know—Jesus Christ changed my life, and He will do the same for you."

DO

value every person highly. We must see every person as one for whom Christ died. If we look down on, or despise any person, we are not worthy to be Christ's servants.

DON'T

be discouraged. Some will reject the Saviour, but keep right on witnessing for Christ.

DO

be concerned. Jesus wept and prayed over lost souls, and so should we.

DO

encourage new converts to confess Christ to others and to join a Bible-believing church at the first opportunity.

Preserve the Harvest

Direct them to a bible-believing church. A church that practices the word of God, where they will be discipled and built up spiritually (John 17:8)
There, they will grow into Christ–like maturity and be equipped for ministry work in the Church and their life mission in the world, in order to magnify God's name. Here they are built up, trained and sent out.

One problem the church is facing today is that many new converts are not discipled. That is why they find it difficult to find or discover their ministry in the church and life mission in the world. Discipleship is very important. It is the duty of the pastor to make sure that his members are developed to Christ-like maturity.

When they are properly discipled, then there will be no need to push them for commitment. When they are mature, they will automatically know what part they are supposed to play in the church. Every one of us has a ministry to fulfill in the church and a life mission to accomplish in the world. When this is properly done, the members will be focused and have direction in life. They will know what they are after.

The early church understood this and they practiced it which is why they were able to spread the gospel very far.

In **Acts 4:8-12,**

"Then Peter, filled with the Holy Ghost, said unto them, Ye rulers of the people, and elders of Israel, If we this day be examined of the good deed done to the impotent man, by what means he is made whole; Be it known unto you all, and to all the people of Israel, that by the name of Jesus Christ of Nazareth, whom ye crucified, whom God raised from the dead, even by him doth this man stand here before you whole. This is the stone which was set at naught of you builders, which is become the head of the corner. Neither is there salvation in any other: for there is none other name under heaven given among men, whereby we must be saved."

Peter used the opportunity that was given to him to proclaim Christ to the leaders and elders that were gathered in Jerusalem. Because of the time they had spent with Jesus, coupled with the power of the Holy Spirit, the people were amazed at the boldness and composure of Peter.

"Now when they saw the boldness of Peter and John, and perceived that they were unlearned and ignorant men, they marveled; and they took knowledge of them, that they had been with Jesus." - **Acts 4:13**

You too can do the same if you are willing to be discipled and receive the power of the Holy Spirit. Your educational background is not a barrier to proclaiming the gospel.

Our Approach to Evangelism

In Corinthians 1:28, Apostle Paul explained to the people that as they went from one town to the other, they told everyone about Christ. At the same time warning and teaching the people with the wisdom that God gave them.
Hence, telling us that we also need heavenly wisdom to proclaim the good news.

In addition, we are to preach the Word in season and out of season. That means we have to do it when it is convenient and when it is not so convenient. Apostle Paul was a man of mission. He was always on the move, whether in sickness or good health.

> *"Iam debtor both to the Greeks, and to the Barbarians; both to the wise, and to the unwise.*
> *So, as much as in me is, I am ready to preach the gospel to you that are at Rome also.*
> *For I am not ashamed of the gospel of Christ: for it is the power of God unto salvation to everyone that believeth; to the Jew first, and also to the Greek.*

Here, Apostle Paul made three personal statements concerning his desire to preach the gospel in Rome.

First in verse 14: **I am bound (a debtor or under obligation)**.To Apostle Paul, it was not optional for him to preach the word of God. It is not like some believers today, to them evangelism is optional.

Secondly in verse 15: **I am eager (ready)**, to Apostle Paul, he was ready at anytime to preach. He made use of every available opportunity that God gave him. He made good use of every open door. What is our attitude today, many are not ready to do it even when they see an open door to preach. We should imitate Paul in this so that we can fulfill the heart desire of Christ.

Thirdly in verse 16: **I am not ashamed-(Rome was a very civilized place).** Rome was a place that people in those days wanted to visit at least once in their lifetime. Apostle Paul was not ready to go as a tourist but as an Evangelist. Many believers today are ashamed to preach the gospel. Some are ashamed because they cannot communicate with good English.

However, when we understand that God sent only begotten Son Jesus to die for us, we will not be ashamed and unwilling to tell others about Jesus and His saving grace to a dying world.
We need to be committed to this great commission that Jesus gave to us and our lives and churches will not remain the same.

CHAPTER SIX

INVEST IN THE KINGDOM

To invest means to put in a lot of **time, effort** or **money,** in order to make something succeed.

The three key words here are: time, money and effort.

What do we understand by time? Time refers to minutes, hours, days, years etc. When you invest time in the Kingdom of God, you are willing to spend minutes, hours, days and years to see that it advances. You spend minutes, hours, days and years to see that souls are won into the Kingdom of God, believers are maturing in Christ, the kingdom of darkness is being de-populated and the children of God are flourishing. These are your concerns and priority. In the midst of tight schedules, we have to invest time to do things which will promote the Kingdom of God.

When I talk of money, I am referring to currency, in the form of coins and notes. It is also your wealth which includes property and material possessions. Therefore you are willing to spend your coins and notes as well as other material goods to see that the Kingdom of God is advancing, souls are being won to the Kingdom of God and your wealth is positively influencing others in the body of Christ.

By effort, I mean the mental or physical energy that is needed to do something. It is also an attempt to do something, especially when it involves a lot of hard work or determination. Advancing the Kingdom of God requires our willingness to use mental and physical energy.

Avenues of Investment

If someone does not invest in a company by buying shares, he cannot be expecting dividends at the end of the year from that company. Many are not in partnership with God concerning His Kingdom and are demanding for dividends from same. What are the avenues by which you can partner with God? There are three major ways which I will want to discuss here.

(1) Giving to support the propagation of the Gospel
(2) Praying for others
(3) Being involved with the propagation of the Gospel

1. Giving to support the Gospel

Tithes and Offerings

Paying of tithes and giving offerings is a way to commit to God. When you pay your tithes and give offerings, you certainly commit (dedicate) your finances to God. It is your way of acknowledging God for giving you power to earn the money. When you do this, God is committed to fulfill His promises which accompany tithes and offering, to you.

While tithe is the mandatory first ten percent of your income, offering is the freewill giving of your own volition. No particular amount or percentage is required or mandated. But note that the quality of your offerings determines your harvest (Luke 6:38). If you do not like what you are receiving, check what you have been giving, because what you give controls what you receive in the Kingdom of God.

"For I am the LORD, I change not; therefore ye sons of Jacob are not consumed. Even from the days of your fathers ye are gone away from mine ordinances, and have not kept them. Return unto me, and I will return unto you, saith the LORD of hosts. But ye said, Wherein shall we return? Will a man rob God? Yet ye have robbed me. But ye say, Wherein have we robbed thee? In tithes and offerings. Ye are cursed with a curse: for ye have robbed me, eventhis whole nation.

*Bring ye all the tithes into the storehouse, that there may
be meat in mine house, and prove me now herewith, saith
the LORD of hosts, if I will not open you the windows of
heaven, and pour you out a blessing, that there shall not be
room enough to receive it.*

*And I will rebuke the devourer for your sakes, and he shall
not destroy the fruits of your ground; neither shall your
vine cast her fruit before the time in the field, saith the
LORD of hosts. And all nations shall call you blessed: for ye
shall be a delightsome land, saith the LORD of hosts."*

-    **Malachi 3:6–12**

God, through Prophet Malachi told the people that they had
strayed from Him and His ordinances. God told them to return
(repent) so that He would return (repent) to them by fulfilling
His promises. When the people asked how they were to return,
the Lord said it was in their tithes and offerings. Beloved, I urge
you to repent as well and begin to pay your tithes. Then God will
fulfill His promises.

In Mal.3:9, anyone who refuses to pay tithe is deemed as
working under a curse. The opposite of blessing is curse. What
curse is being talked about? Let's look at the scriptures.

In Luke 9:16, when Jesus was about to feed the five thousand with five leaves of bread and two fishes, he took the bread and blessed it, and he began to break the bread for the people to eat.

To bless the bread here means to multiply.

Also, in **Genesis 1:28**, the bible says:
"And *God blessed them, and God said unto them, be fruitful, and multiply, and replenish the earth, and subdue it: and have dominion over the fish of the sea and over the fowl of the air, and over every living thing that moves upon the earth)*."

God Himself blessed Adam and Eve and told them to be fruitful, multiply, replenish the earth and subdue it - have dominion. Hence, wc can see that this is the way God blesses. Since the opposite of blessing is curse, we can tell the opposite of fruitfulness, multiplication, replenishing, and dominion. So any Christian who is not paying his or her tithe is walking in the opposite of dominion. He or she will find it difficult to be fruitful, multiply, and dominate. They will be dominated by circumstances. They will go back to the curse that was placed on the ground for the sake of man.

"And unto Adam he said, Because thou hast hearkened unto the voice of thy wife, and hast eaten of the tree, of which I commanded thee, saying, Thou shall not eat of it: cursed is the ground for thy sake; in sorrow shall thou eat of it all the days of thy life; Thorns also and thistles shall it bring forth to thee; and thou shall eat the herb of the field; In the sweat of thy face shall thou eat bread, till thou return unto the ground; for out of it was thou taken: for dust thou art, and unto dust shall thou return)."

- **Gen. 3:17-19**

The person will continue to struggle in life without tangible results, working like an elephant, but eating like ant. He will work, without seeing the fruit of his labor, because he is walking the opposite direction to blessing. The windows of heaven will be shut and devourers will be destroying his means of livelihood.

However, faithfulness in tithes elevates you to walking in God's blessings. The windows of heaven will be opened and God himself will rebuke the devourer for you. You will not experience premature harvest.

A note of warning regards tithes - when you fail in paying one time, and you want to redeem it, a 20%penalty has to be paid in addition to the original tithe.

"And all the tithe of the land, whether of the seed of the land, or of the fruit of the tree, is the LORD's: it is holy unto the LORD. And if a man will at all redeem ought of his tithes, he shall add thereto the fifth part thereof."

- **Leviticus 27: 30–31**

The purpose of the 20% sub charge is to discourage people from meddling with God's money. The moment tithing is missing people make room for the curse to return.

Where to Pay Tithe

If you are not committed to any assembly of believers now, find a local church, where the genuine undiluted Word of God is preached. Be committed and pay your tithes there.

Perhaps you are presently in a church, where the bible is not fully taught, then you are being starved spiritually because you are not receiving spiritual nutrition. Church attendance should teach victorious Christian living. If all you are getting is a feeling of excitement and no tangible word to carry you through from Monday through Saturday, that is a dead church, and you should not put your tithe there.

What should you be looking for in a church?

In order to know what to look for in a local church, we must first understand God's purpose for the church—the body of Christ. There are two outstanding truths about the church. First, "the church of the living God [is] the pillar and foundation of the truth" (1 Timothy 3:15). Second, Christ alone is the head of the church (Ephesians 1:22; 4:15; Colossians 1:18).

In regard to the truth, the local church is a place where the Bible (God's only Truth) has complete authority. The Bible is the only infallible rule of faith and practice (2 Timothy 3:15-17). Therefore, when seeking a church to attend, we should find one where, according to biblical standards, the gospel is preached, sin is condemned, worship is from the heart, the teaching is biblical, and opportunities to minister to others exist.

Consider the model of the early church found in **Acts 2:42-47**, *"They devoted themselves to the apostles' teaching and to the fellowship, to the breaking of bread and to prayer...They broke bread in their homes and ate together with glad and sincere hearts, praising God and enjoying the favor of all the people. And the Lord added to their number daily those who were being saved."*

With regard to the second truth about the church, Christians should attend a local fellowship that declares Christ's headship in all matters of doctrine and practice. No man—whether pastor, priest, or pope—is the head of the church. All men die. How then can the living Church of the living God have a dead head? It cannot. Christ is the church's one supreme authority, and all church leadership, gifts, order, discipline, and worship are appointed through His sovereignty, as found in the Scriptures.

Once these two fundamentals are in place, the rest of the factors (buildings, worship styles, activities, programs, location, etc.) are merely a matter of personal taste. Before even setting foot inside a church, some homework is in order. Doctrinal statements, purpose statements, mission statements, or anything that will give insight into what a church believes should be carefully looked over. Many churches have websites where one can get a feel for what they believe regarding the Bible, God, the Trinity, Jesus Christ, sin, and salvation.

Next, should be visits to the churches that seem to have the fundamentals in place. Attendance at two or three services at each church will be helpful. Any literature they have for visitors should be scrutinized, paying close attention to belief statements. Church evaluation should be based on the principles outlined above. Is the Bible held as the only authority? Is Christ exalted as head of the church? Does the church focus on discipleship? Were you led to worship God? What types of ministries does the church involve itself in? Was the message biblical and evangelical? How was the fellowship? You also need to feel comfortable—were you made to feel welcome? Is the congregation comprised of true worshippers?

Finally, remember that no church is perfect. At best, it is filled with saved sinners, whose flesh and spirits are continually at war. Also, do not forget the importance of prayer. Praying about the church God would have you attend is crucial throughout the decision-making process.

Clergy Support

Supporting the church (men of God) with our resources so that the preaching of the gospel is not hindered is a noble cause.

Now think about this. Jesus had 12 disciples, who accompanied Him to every town He went. They were His companions. They were always with Him. Have you ever wondered how Jesus was able to take care of these full grown men? Many of His disciples had families, yet Jesus took care of them for 3 ½ years. That is great. Let me put it in today's terms – He had 12 men on His payroll. These disciples left houses, brothers, sisters, fathers, mothers, wife, children to follow Jesus (Mk. 10: 28 – 30). Remember when Jesus called James and John in Mt. 4:21, the bible says they left their father, Zebedee.

Without a shadow of doubt, it took Jesus a lot of resources to take care of these people and even give to the poor (John. 13:29)The question now is: Where was Jesus getting all the resources from?

> ***"And Joanna the wife of Chuza Herod's steward, and Susanna, and many others, which ministered unto him of their substance)."*** Luke 8:3

The bible says that this set of people, contributed from whatever resources God had blessed them with in order to support Jesus and His disciples. These were people, who could not follow Jesus around physically, so they supported and sustained His ministerial trips from their pockets. They were businessmen and women, workers etc. They made it possible for Jesus to pay His bills.

The business of seeking and saving the lost requires huge amount of resources. Where will the resources come from? I am happy to say that it will come from you, who are businessmen and women, entrepreneurs, paid workers, believers, who God has blessed with these resources. The gospel needs to be preached by every means available needing the printing of tracts, crusades, radio and TV broadcasts etc. It takes good money to go on air, preaching on TV so as to reach a wider audience. It takes money to build a good place of worship. Money is essential to pay the staff on church payroll. When there is provision in God's house, all these things can be taken care of.

During one of Jesus' earthly crusades, a need to feed the multitudes arose and a young man, who had nothing but five barley loaves, and two small fishes volunteered to meet that need. From that little provision, there was excess.(John 6: 1-13)

The bible also tells the story of the woman with the alabaster box, who poured expensive perfume on Jesus. Our Lord Jesus received her gesture with much gratitude and commended her unusual faith.(Luke 7:36-48)

The Philippians' Church ministered to the needs of Apostle Paul as recorded in the epistle written to them. He says:

"But I rejoiced in the Lord greatly, that now at the last your care of me hath flourished again; wherein ye were also careful, but ye lacked opportunity."

Further down, he crowned it with the popular verse 19:

"But my God shall supply all your need according to his riches in glory by Christ Jesus."
Philippians 4:10, 19

Giving is not only an act, it is also a ministry and Apostle Paul encouraged the Corinthian church to share in this ministry (2 Cor. 8:6-8.) I encourage everyone – young, old, rich, poor, to get involved in the ministry of giving.

The Love of Money

Unfortunately, not everyone will give as they should despite having abundance. One reason is that the love of money has hardened the hearts of many from giving freely. To be a genuine giver, the love of money must be far from you. The love of money hinders effective giving. Here are a few scriptures on the love of money.

"Jesus said to him, 'If you wish to be complete, go and sell your possessions and give to the poor, and you will have treasure in heaven; and come, follow Me.' But when the young man heard this statement, he went away grieving; for he was one who owned much property. And Jesus said to His disciples, "Truly I say to you, it is hard for a rich man to enter the kingdom of heaven.

"Again I say to you, it is easier for a camel to go through the eye of a needle, than for a rich man to enter the kingdom of God." When the disciples heard this, they were very astonished and said, 'Then who can be saved?' And looking at them Jesus said to them, "With people this is impossible, but with God all things are possible."

-   **Matthew 19:21-26**

"But the worries of the world, and the deceitfulness of riches, and the desires for other things enter in and choke the word, and it becomes unfruitful."

-   **Mark 4:19**

"For what does it profit a man to gain the whole world, and forfeit his soul?"

-   **Mark 8:36**

"But those who want to get rich fall into temptation and a snare and many foolish and harmful desires which plunge men into ruin and destruction. For the love of money is a root of all sorts of evil, and some by longing for it have wandered away from the faith and

pierced themselves with many griefs. But flee from these things, you man of God, and pursue righteousness, godliness, faith, love, perseverance and gentleness."

\-   **1 Timothy 6:9-11**

"Come now, you rich, weep and howl for your miseries which are coming upon you. Your riches have rotted and your garments have become moth-eaten. Your gold and your silver have rusted; and their rust will be a witness against you and will consume your flesh like fire. It is in the last days that you have stored up your treasure! Behold, the pay of the laborers who mowed your fields, and which has been withheld by you, cries out against you; and the outcry of those who did the harvesting has reached the ears of the Lord of Sabaoth. You have lived luxuriously on the earth and led a life of wanton pleasure; you have fattened your hearts in a day of slaughter. You have condemned and put to death the righteous man; he does not resist you."

\-   ***James 5:1-6***

Biblical View on Planning

In order to be a good giver, you have to be financially prudent and plan spending wisely. One profound bible record on planning is the story of the ten virgins, who were waiting to meet the bridegroom. The bible calls five of them foolish and the other five prudent. The foolish took their lamps without extra oil but the prudent did so. You can read the entire account in **Matthew 25:1-13**. The five were wise because they planned for unforeseen circumstances and took extra oil along.

Here are some scriptures on the importance of planning.

"Let Pharaoh take action to appoint overseers in charge of the land, and let him exact a fifth of the produce of the land of Egypt in the seven years of abundance. "Then let them gather all the food of these good years that are coming, and store up the grain for food in the cities under Pharaoh's authority, and let them guard it. "Let the food become as a reserve for the land for the seven years of famine which will occur in the land of Egypt, so that the land will not perish during the famine."

- **Genesis 41:34-36**

"Go to the ant, o sluggard, observe her ways and be wise, which, having no chief, officer or ruler, prepares her food in the summer and gathers her provision in the harvest."

- **Proverbs 6:6-8**

"A wise man thinks ahead; a fool doesn't, and even brags about it!"

- **Proverbs 13:16**

"Without consultation, plans are frustrated, but with many counselors they succeed."

- **Proverbs 15:22**

"Prepare plans by consultation, and make war by wise guidance."

- **Proverbs 20:18**

"The plans of the diligent lead surely to advantage, but everyone who is hasty comes surely to poverty."

-   Proverbs 21:5

"The prudent sees the evil and hides himself, but the naive go on, and are punished for it."

-   Proverbs 22:3

"By wisdom a house is built, and by understanding it is established; and by knowledge the rooms are filled with all precious and pleasant riches."

-   Proverbs 24:3-4

"Prepare your work outside and make it ready for yourself in the field; afterwards, then, build your house."

-   Proverbs 24:27

"For which one of you, when he wants to build a tower, does not first sit down and calculate the cost to see if he has enough to complete it? "Otherwise, when he has laid a foundation and is not able to finish, all who observe it begin to ridicule him, saying, 'This man began to build and was not able to finish."

-   Luke 14:28-30

Planning Your Finances

"And it shall come to pass in the harvest that you shall give one-fifth to Pharaoh. Four-fifths shall be your own, as seed for the field and for your food, for those of your households and as food for your little ones."(NKJV)

-   Genesis 47:24

Going by the above scripture, one-fifth of one's income should be given as tithe; the remaining four-fifth is for the individual. This four-fifth will be used for seed, yourself, your household and children.

Suggested Financial Breakdown (%)

1) Tithe   10%

2) Seed   15%

3) Household   20%

4) Self   10%

5) Savings   10%

6) Children   25%

7) Others (offering, gifts, etc.)10%

Analysis of Breakdown

Item 1, which is tithe, is ten percent of your earnings and it is not negotiable. It is the tenth that belongs to God, Who gives us power, strength and enablement to make wealth.

Item 2, which is seed, should be sown into the lives of your natural and spiritual parents. You can also sow some into the Kingdom of God. The amounts you give to parents and sow totally depend on you.

Item 3, for your household expenses, should be shared among rent, feeding and paying of utilities amongst other immediate family concerns.

Item 4, for your personal needs, is exactly as it says, for you to buy your personal effects.

Item 5, savings, should be for emergency and investment opportunities.

The sixth item is meant for children school fees and upkeep.

Lastly, the remaining ten percent is reserved for offering, buying of gifts, and can also be given to support the work of the ministry.

This is not a rigid plan and you can make some adjustments where necessary, as it applies to your particular situation. I hope it will at least gives you an insight into how to manage your finances to avoid wasteful expenditure.

Assurances of Provision

Some believers are afraid to give. They think that if they give out of the little they have, they will not be able to meet their needs and obligations. Many have hindered themselves by this belief and have been unable to overcome poverty or living from hand to mouth.

Many scripture passages assure us that God will surely meet our needs. God has promised provision and He does not lie. Here are a few scripture verses that can encourage our hearts:

"Then Elijah said to her, "Do not fear; go, do as you have said, but make me a little bread cake from it first and bring it out to me, and afterward you may make one for yourself and for your son. For thus says the Lord God of Israel, 'The bowl of flour shall not be exhausted, nor shall the jar of oil be empty, until the day that the Lord sends rain on the face of the earth.'"

So she went and did according to the word of Elijah, and she and he and her household ate for many days. The bowl of flour was not exhausted nor did the jar of oil become empty, according to the word of the Lord which He spoke through Elijah."

- **1 Kings 17:13-16**

"I have been young and now I am old, yet I have not seen the righteous forsaken or his descendants begging bread."

- **Psalm 37:25**

"Do not worry then, saying, 'What will we eat?' or 'What will we drink?' or 'What will we wear for clothing?' For the Gentiles eagerly seek all these things; for your heavenly Father knows that you need all these things."

- **Matthew 6:31-32**

"If you then, being evil, know how to give good gifts to your children, how much more will your Father who is in heaven give what is good to those who ask Him!"

- **Matthew 7:11**

"Indeed, the very hairs of your head are all numbered. Do not fear; you are more valuable than many sparrows."

- **Luke 12:7**

"And God is able to make all grace abound to you, so that always having all sufficiency in everything; you may have abundance for every good deed..."

- **2 Corinthians 9:8**

"And my God will supply all your needs according to His riches in glory in Christ Jesus."

- **Philippians 4:19**

You have to be part of this business of seeking and saving those who are lost. Seeking them involve resources (money). Where will the finance come from? It should be you. God blessed you for this reason.

In Deut. 8:18

It is God that has given you the power to make that money so that He can establish His covenant on earth. And part of that agreement (Covenant) is that you will also obey the command to go into the world to win souls for the kingdom of God. John. 17:18-20-.

In Mt. 10:40 – 42

He that receives you receives me, and he that receives me receives him that sent me. He that receives a prophet in the name of a prophet shall receive a prophet's reward; and he that receives a righteous man in the name of a righteous man shall receive a righteous man's reward. And whosoever shall give to drink unto one of these little ones a cup of cold water only in the name of a disciple, verily I say unto you, he shall in no wise lose his reward.

Jesus Christ stated that when you welcome a prophet, you will be rewarded. When you give a cup of cold water to the least of His followers, you will surely be rewarded.

My Brothers and sisters in Christ, you don't know why things are going the way they are? Let's look at a very important scripture.

Haggai 1: 3 – 11 ***Then came the word of the LORD by Haggai the prophet, saying, Is it time for you, O ye, to dwell in your ceiled houses, and this house lie waste? Now therefore thus saith the LORD of hosts; Consider your ways. Ye have sown much, and bring in little; ye eat, but ye have not enough; ye drink, but ye are not filled with drink; ye clothe you, but there is none warm; and he that earneth wages to put it into a bag with holes. Thus saith the LORD of hosts; Consider your ways. Go up to the mountain, and bring wood, and build the house; and I will take pleasure in it, and I will be glorified, saith the LORD. Ye looked for much, and, lo it came to little; and when ye brought it home, I did blow upon it. Why? saith the LORD of hosts. Because of mine house that is waste, and ye run every man unto his own house. Therefore the heaven over you is stayed from dew, and the earth is stayed from her fruit. And I called for a drought upon the land, and upon the mountains, and upon the corn, and upon the new wine, and upon the oil, and upon that which the ground bringeth forth, and upon men, and upon cattle, and upon all the labor of the hands.***

There are many that live in luxurious houses while the house of God is in ruin. They are busy taking care of their personal needs, while they don't have any contribution to the house of God. You need to be committed to building the house of God. Make the house of God conducive for worship. God will bless you for your contribution to the beautification of His house.

2.   Praying for Others

"Epaphras, who is one of you, a servant of Christ, salutes you, always laboring fervently for you in prayers, that ye may stand perfect and complete in all the will of God. For I bear him record, that he hath a great zeal for you, and them that are in Laodicea, and them in Hierapolis."

-   **Col. 4: 12-13**

In the bible reading above, Apostle Paul spoke highly of a certain disciple, Epaphras by name, who fervently engaged in the ministry of intercession for the brethren. This brother was always praying for the Colossian church and other Christians from Laodicea and Hierapolis.

Someone might say, Pastor Simon, I do not have resources to give; you can be part of the prayer ministry. Feel free to meet your church pastor about your desire to join the prayer ministry. Or if there is none existent, God can use you to start one right there in your local assembly.

I would like to say a few things briefly about the ministry of prayer (intercession).

In **Job 16:21**, the bible says this about intercession, *"Oh, that one might plead for a man with God, as a man pleaded for his neighbor!"*

What is intercession? It is the action of intervening on behalf of another. What is intercessory prayer? Intercessory prayer is the act of praying on behalf of others. The role of mediator in prayer was prevalent in the Old Testament, in the cases of Abraham, Moses, David, Samuel, Hezekiah, Elijah, Jeremiah, Ezekiel, and Daniel. Christ is pictured in the New Testament as the ultimate intercessor, and because of this, all Christian prayer becomes intercession since it is offered to God through and by Christ. Because of Jesus' mediation, we can now intercede in prayer on behalf of other Christians or FOR THE LOST, asking God to grant their requests according to His will. "For there is one God and one mediator between God and men, the man Christ Jesus"(1 Timothy 2:5). "Who is he that condemns? Christ Jesus, who died—more than that, who was raised to life—is at the right hand of God and is also interceding for us" (Romans 8:34). We are to pray for the lost soul to be brought into the Kingdom of God. It is our duty to intercede for the believers until Christ is formed in them.

Prayer is a primary and important prerequisite in the work of the Kingdom. We need to pray for souls to be won and established. We need to pray for people to be delivered from the bondages the enemy has used to hold them bound for years. We need prayer to keep the fire and zeal of God's work burning in our hearts. This is why it is necessary for all to be involved in praying. But more so, for those that can commit to stay in the place of prayers for the work, their reward cannot be overlooked by heaven.

(3) Being involved with the propagation of the Gospel

We can be involved in the physical work of evangelism by joining those, who God has called to do the job. We can go from house to house to meet people where they are in order to tell them the good news of the Kingdom. We can also do one-on-one personal evangelism. On another hand, we can go for short or long term mission work with missionaries in the fields. Time and energy can be spent to ensure that souls are won to the Kingdom of God. Many mission fields are in serious need of professionals to help with health, career, counseling, educational and other humanitarian needs necessary in ministering to new converts in most interior villages.

Money is also needed to take care of many of the needs of both stationed missionaries and converts. Those who are well-to-do and can afford to send financial resources can also do, if they are unable to go to the mission fields in person. There is always a reward for soul winning for those who give to the cause, those who pray as well as those who are involved physically. If you desire to know how to be effective in soul winning, please read the chapter (five), on telling others about Christ.

"And how will they preach unless they are commissioned *and* sent [for that purpose]? Just as it is written *and* forever remains written, "How beautiful are the feet of those who bring good news of good things!" **Romans 10:15** (AMP)

My prayer is that your labour in the Kingdom will be rewarded in Jesus name.

FINAL WORDS

There are rewards for our labour here on earth and when we get to heaven after our sojourn here on earth. There are crowns waiting for us in heaven. I want to briefly talk about some of those crowns.

1) Crown of righteousness: 2Timothy 4:7-8; (***I have fought the good fight, I have finished the race, I have kept the faith. Finally, there is laid up for me the crown of righteousness, which the Lord, the righteous Judge, will give to me on that Day, and not to me only but also to all who have loved His appearing***). This crown will be given to those that have been able to fight the good fight of faith and were able to keep the faith. They did not lose their faith during the process of fighting the good fight of faith. It is also for those that have been able to complete their race; that is assignment given to them. Every Christian has a purpose to serve during his/her life time. This purpose is not yours but God's purpose. Acts 13:36, talks about King David serving the purpose of God for his generation then he fell asleep (NIV). Your generation is the people that live in your life time. Your generation never passes away until you exit this world. You are to

affect positively or be of help to those who are still living in your lifetime. Your purpose is the reason why you were created. God created you for a purpose and it is your duty to discover this purpose. I encourage you to discover your purpose and live a purpose driven life. This crown is not for those who depend upon their own sense of righteousness or of their own works.

2) Crown of life: James 1:12(***Blessed [happy, spiritually prosperous, favored by God] is the man who is steadfast under trial and perseveres when tempted; for when he has passed the test and been approved, he will receive the [victor's] crown of life which the Lord has promised to those who love Him***) AMP. This crown is for those that were steadfast under trial and perseveres in temptation. You need to learn how to be steadfast in trial. When we are being tried, we should take our stand for God and never be double minded. You should be strong in the Lord when tried, for this is the way you can overcome. Daniel 11:32 says that they that know their God shall be strong and do exploit. You should know God for yourself and this will make you to be strong. Revelation 2:10 "***Do not fear any of those things which you are about to suffer. Indeed, the devil is about to throw some of you into prison, that you may be tested, and you will have***

tribulation ten days. Be faithful until death, and I will give you the crown of life." This crown is for all believers, but is especially dear to those who endure sufferings, who bravely confront persecution for Jesus, even to the point of death

3) Crown of glory: 1 Peter 5:3-4(*not lording it over those assigned to your care [do not be arrogant or overbearing], but be examples [of Christian living] to the flock [set a pattern of integrity for your congregation]. And when the Chief Shepherd (Christ) appears, you will receive the [conqueror's] unfading crown of glory)* AMP. The bible says we should not lord it over those that have been set under us. Do not be arrogant or overbearing over those who follow you. Arrogance as earlier defined means someone behaving in a rude way, because they think they are very important. An arrogant person will always have an unteachable spirit. They never want to learn from others. To be overbearing means unpleasantly overpowering, often trying to control the behavior of other people and too confident and too determined to tell other people what to do. Do you fall into such category, please repent so that you can receive your crown of glory when the Chief Shepherd shall come. How can we be an example? Apostle Paul encouraged Timothy to be an example to believers in word, in conduct, in love, in spirit, in faith and in purity. So we should be an

example to believers in word, in conduct, in love, in spirit, in faith and in purity.

4) Imperishable crown. 1 Corinthians 9:24-25(***Do you not know that in a race all the runners run [their very best to win], but only one receives the prize? Run [your race] in such a way that you may seize the prize and make it yours! Now every athlete who [goes into training and] competes in the games is disciplined and exercises self-control in all things. They do it to win a crown that withers, but we [do it to receive] an imperishable [crown that cannot wither].*** I encourage you to run to win this imperishable crown. To win the race, you have to be disciplined and exercise self-control in all things that you do. Apostle Paul told Timothy in 2 Timothy 2: 3-5 that we must endure hardship as a good soldier of Christ. He said any one who engages in warfare does not entangle himself with the affairs of this life. Why? He said so that we can please Him who enlisted him as a soldier. So for us to win, we must endure hardship and as soldiers of Christ, we must not entangle ourselves with the affairs of this life. In verse 5, he compared us with an athlete who compete in any game must compete according to the rules of the game in other to win and be crowned. So we must compete according to the rules. The kingdom of God operates by principles and divine laws. If

we work against any law consciously or unconsciously, we experience the negative side of the law.

The God factor

I want to use this opportunity to talk about the God factor. By God Factor, I mean because God has said it, that when you are committed to Him, you will share testimony, count it done. God will not fail in His Word.

In Micah 5:2, the bible says *"**But you, Bethlehem Ephrathah, though you are little among the thousands of Judah, Yet out of you shall come forth to Me the One to be Ruler in Israel, Whose goings forth are from of old, from everlasting.**"* This prophecy came to pass in Luke 2:1-7 *"**And it came to pass in those days that a decree went out from Caesar Augustus that all the world should be registered. 2 This census first took place while Quirinius was governing Syria. 3 So all went to be registered, everyone to his own city. Joseph also went up from Galilee, out of the city of Nazareth, into Judea, to the city of David, which is called Bethlehem, because he was of the house and lineage of David, 5 to be registered with Mary, his betrothed wife, who was with child. 6 So it was, that while they were there, the days were completed for her to be delivered. 7 And she brought forth her firstborn Son, and wrapped Him in swaddling clothes, and laid Him in a manger, because there** *was no room for them in the inn.*" Can you see the wonder working God in action? The word came through prophet Micah many years ago that out of Bethlehem will come forth the ruler of Israel and it came to pass in the gospel of Luke. Mary and Joseph were in Nazareth with pregnancy of the baby Jesus and God moved Caesar Augustus to make a decree for everyone to go to their home town for census, this was what took Joseph to live Nazareth to Bethlehem for registration. And the Bible says, "While they were there, the days were completed for her to be delivered" If not because of the decree, Jesus could have been born in Nazareth which may have made God a liar. But God is not a liar. So whatever that is needed to be done for this word of God to come to pass in your life will be done in Jesus name.

Again in 1 Kings 12:15, "So the king did not listen to the people; for the turn *of events* was from the Lord, that He might fulfill His word, which the Lord had spoken by Ahijah the Shilonite to Jeroboam the son of Nebat**."** This was the fulfillment of the prophecy given by God through prophet Ahijah to Jeroboam during the reign of King Solomon. What was the prophecy? **1 Kings 11:11**"Therefore the Lord said to Solomon, "Because you have done this, and have not kept My covenant and My statutes, which I have commanded you, I will surely tear the kingdom away from you and give it to your servant." **1 kings 11:29-31** "Now it happened at that time, when Jeroboam went out of Jerusalem that the prophet Ahijah the Shilonite met him on the way; and he had clothed himself with a new garment, and the two *were* alone in the field. 30 Then Ahijah took hold of the new garment that *was* on him, and tore it *into* twelve pieces. 31 And he said to Jeroboam, "Take for yourself ten pieces, for thus says the Lord, the God of Israel: 'Behold, I will tear the kingdom out of the hand of Solomon and will give ten tribes to you." We can see from the scriptures above that king Rehoboam rejecting the counsel of the older counselors was from God. God turned the event to favor His word He spoke through the prophet. So events will be turned by God to fulfill this word in your life in Jesus name. Whatever event that needs to be turned, it will turn for your favor in Jesus name.

Finally, Hebrews 6:17-19, "[17] Thus God, determining to show more abundantly to the heirs of promise the immutability of His counsel, confirmed *it* by an oath, [18] that by two immutable things, in which it *is* impossible for God to lie, we might have strong consolation, who have fled for refuge to lay hold of the hope set before *us*. [19] This *hope* we have as an anchor of the soul, both sure and steadfast, and which enters the *Presence* behind the veil," God did two things here: He made a promise and confirmed the promise with an oath. How did God swear an oath to Abraham? Genesis 15:9-10, So He said to him, "Bring Me a three-year-old heifer, a three-year-old female goat, a three-year-old ram, a turtledove, and a young pigeon." [10] Then he brought all these to Him and cut them in two, down the middle, and placed each piece opposite the other; but he did not cut the birds in two. Then verse 17, "And it came to pass, when the sun went down and it was dark, that behold, there appeared a smoking oven and a burning torch that passed between those pieces." When Abraham offered the sacrifice to God by cutting the animals into pieces, he placed the piece opposite the other and in verse 17; the Spirit of the Lord went in between the dead animals. What is the significance of this? God was telling Abraham that if I fail my promise, I will die like these animals and you know God cannot die. How do I know this was what happened? Jeremiah 34:18 says, and I will give the men who have transgressed My covenant, who have not performed the words of the covenant which they made before Me, **when they cut the calf in two and passed between the parts of it.** This was how oath was made during this time. By passing between the parts of the dead animals, they are saying that if I fail in this oath, I will die like these animals.

 Do your part by obeying all the instructions he has given to you in this book and wait patiently for him to fulfill his promises.

> **Deuteronomy 7: 9**
>
> *Understand therefore, that the Lord your God is indeed God. He is the faithful God who keeps His covenant for a thousand generations and constantly loves those who love Him and obey His commands.(NLT)*

God is faithful and He will keep His promises and covenants.

> **Hebrews 10:23**
>
> *Without wavering, let us hold tightly to the hope we say we have, for God can be trusted to keep His promise.(NLT).* God can be trusted to fulfill His word.

God *is* not a man, that He should lie, nor a son of man, that He should repent. Has He said, and will He not do? Or has He spoken, and will He not make it good? Numbers 23:19. God will certainly bring His word to pass. **God said it, I believe it and that settles it.**

Some of My Testimonies

In January 1997, when God called me into ministry, there was a need to go to a Bible College, there was no one to help for my family said they cannot sponsor me in Bible College. God came to my aid by giving me scholarship through an Australian who decided to pay for my fees.

When I was through, I came to Lagos and picked up a job with a ministry. In 2001 God asked me what I was waiting for in the area of marriage. I told Him I do not have the money for my wedding. God told me not to say I do not have money that I should go ahead with the marriage plans. That was how God helped me during and after my marriage.

After some years I change to another ministry because I was looking for a place where there is structure to serve and learn. When I was with this ministry, things were not still going well because the ministry could not fulfill its promises made. Then in 2007, I cried to God, asking Him if that was how I will continue. God told me that He has seen my commitment and also aware that they do not recognize my service there. He said I should go to a Seminary to further ministry education. I told Him that I cannot afford the fees, He promised to send me a helper. In 2008 God connected me with an American; Dr. Dan Finch of the blessed memory. He offered to pay my way through Seminary. That was how I got my Bachelor of Arts in Theology.

Again in 2009 God asked me to write a book on,' **How the Righteous will Flourish in these Last Days'**. As I completed the writing I told Him to give me the money to publish the book and He promised to send me somebody who will give the money to do it. After about four months the man came and gave me some money that assisted me in publishing the book in 2011.

Again in 2014, I desired to do a Master's program in Christian Counseling and I searched for many schools who offer the course and at the same time willing to offer me scholarship. I applied to many schools and about five agreed to offer half scholarship which was running into almost a million naira ($3450) which I could not afford. I began to pray that God should send me somebody who can help me out. After many months of praying and waiting, miraculously one of the schools finally agreed to give me full scholarship.

I attribute all these to the commitment I have given to God through my service in His vineyard. My work in the ministry has never been on the basis of been paid good salary, but my desire to do His will and serve His purpose for my generation.

CONCLUSION

Nothing compares with commitment to God and it most assuredly comes with blessings from heaven above, even though in our time, it seems many believers' lives paint a contrary picture. The Bible says man looks at the outward appearance while God searches the heart. The truth about commitment is that it is not just about what you do; your heart matters. Perhaps, many believers have questionable motives and are not quite as faithful as God requires of them. Over all, God is the ultimate judge of man's every action and motive.

We have seen from both the Old and the New Testament of men and women who were committed to God, how they did it and the blessing(s) that follow. They gave their lives to God and His service. They made a total allegiance to God, His work and God's people. They obeyed divine instructions that were given by men and women of God. They subdue kingdoms, worked righteousness, stopped the mouth of lions, quenched the violence of fire, escape the edge of sword, out of weakness they were made strong. They fellowshipped and shared bread together as a family because of their covenant relationship with Jesus. Today we can do more than they did and obtain more blessings as they had because of what Jesus Christ has done for us. The Bible says we should imitate those who through faith and patience inherited the promise (Hebrews 6:12).

Notwithstanding, with a foundation of right intention and diligence I can personally testify that commitment to God pays. When you do not seek the praise of men, not involved in eye service and are loyal to the One who called you. My life has been a testimony since the day I surrendered my heart to Christ, passionately embracing His love and His work.

When I encountered Christ in 1993, I had a genuine desire to know God. I spent hours upon hours reading and studying my Bible. I attended church services whenever the doors of the church were open, participating in virtually all church activities. This zeal contributed immensely to my spiritual growth. The pastor and elders took notice of it and before long, I was appointed youth leader of our local assembly. I also believe that my commitment contributed to the scholarship I got towards my two-year Bible College education. My work with the church was never at any point centered round monetary gains -only unquenchable desire to serve God. Commitment also connected me to a total stranger, who sponsored me through my four-year program in West Africa Theological Seminary.

I want to use this opportunity to advise those who desire to have outstanding testimonies, to be committed to God with a genuine heart and remain faithful in their commitment. God is an unfailing rewarder, who will reward you for all your service.

Commitment Pays!

About the Author

Simon Osadebamwen Osamwonyi is a Pastor, Teacher, Counselor and Administrator, with a burden to disciple and mentor believers in order for them to grow in the full knowledge of Jesus Christ.

He is a graduate of All Nations for Christ Bible Institute International, Benin City, Nigeria. He also holds a Bachelor's degree from the West Africa Theological Seminary, Lagos Nigeria and a Masters' degree in Christian counseling from Canon Research Theological Seminary (formerly North Central Theological Seminary), Minnesota, United States of America.

He is happily married to Beauty Osasere and they are blessed with three children- Efosa, Obosa and Esosa.

About the Book

 The book, **Understanding the power of commitment to God** is borne out of the author's quest to understand why some longstanding Christians have no evident fruit of commitment in their lives. While seeking God's face, God's clear response to him was that **anyone who is committed to Him (God) will always have a testimony to share**. The six keys which God opened Pastor Simon's eyes to, are presented in this book. These are principles we as believers are to live by in these last days.